故園憶

庚寅中秋
韓馨汝題

《故园画忆系列》编委会

名誉主任： 韩启德

主　　任： 邵　鸿

委　　员：（按姓氏笔画为序）

万　捷	王秋桂	方李莉	叶培贵
刘魁立	况　晗	严绍璗	吴为山
范贻光	范　芳	孟　白	邵　鸿
岳庆平	郑培凯	唐晓峰	曹兵武

故园画忆系列
MEMORY OF THE OLD
Home in Sketches

北京胡同记忆
Hutongs of Old Beijing

戴程松　绘画 撰文
Sketches & Notes by Dai Chengsong

学苑出版社
ACADEMY PRESS

图书在版编目（CIP）数据

北京胡同记忆 / 戴程松绘、撰文. —北京：学苑出版社，2012.2

（故园画忆系列）

ISBN 978-7-5077-3974-9

Ⅰ. ①北… Ⅱ. ①戴… Ⅲ. ①建筑画：写生画-作品集-中国-现代 Ⅳ. ①TU204

中国版本图书馆CIP数据核字（2012）第021549号

出 版 人：	孟　白
出版发行：	学苑出版社
社　　址：	北京市丰台区南方庄2号院1号楼
邮政编码：	100079
网　　址：	www.book001.com
电子信箱：	xueyuanpress@163.com
销售电话：	010-67601101（营销部）、67603091（总编室）
经　　销：	全国新华书店
印 刷 厂：	三河市灵山红旗印刷厂
开本尺寸：	889×1194　1/24
印　　张：	9.5
字　　数：	100千字
图　　幅：	195幅
印　　数：	3000册
版　　次：	2012年3月北京第1版
印　　次：	2016年3月北京第3次印刷
定　　价：	68.00元

目　　录

胡同缘（序）　　　　　　　　　　戴程松

一　老店铺旧址　　　　　　　　　　1
东城区
门楼胡同 3 号、5 号　老当铺旧址　　3
东四四条 86 号　老店铺旧址　　　　4
崇文区
西兴隆街　老商街（之一）　　　　　5
西兴隆街　老商街（之二）　　　　　6
西兴隆街　老商街（之三）　　　　　7
鲜鱼口街　老商街（之一）　　　　　8
鲜鱼口街　老商街（之二）　　　　　9
鲜鱼口街　老商街（之三）　　　　　10
南晓顺胡同　老商铺旧址　　　　　　11
西打磨厂街　老店街（之一）　　　　12
西打磨厂街　老店街（之二）　　　　13
大江胡同　老商铺旧址　　　　　　　14
布巷子胡同　老商号旧址　　　　　　15
宣武区
廊坊头条　金店旧址　　　　　　　　16
大栅栏街　老商街　　　　　　　　　17
廊坊二条　老商街（之一）　　　　　18
廊坊二条　老商街（之二）　　　　　19
小椿树胡同　老店铺旧址　　　　　　20
培智胡同　老店铺旧址　　　　　　　21

校场口胡同 41 号　老店铺旧址　　　22
校场口胡同 57 号　老店铺旧址　　　23
棕树斜街 1 号　老店铺旧址　　　　　24
杨梅竹斜街 31 号　老店铺旧址　　　25
钱市胡同　老钱庄旧址　　　　　　　26
朱家胡同 45 号 "临春楼" 妓院旧址　27
朱茅胡同 9 号 "聚宝茶室" 妓院旧址　28
小力胡同 25 号 "蕊香楼" 妓院旧址　29

二　名人故居、会馆、王府、宗祠　31
东城区
豆腐池胡同 15 号　毛泽东故居　　　33
东四八条 71 号　叶圣陶故居　　　　34
后圆恩寺胡同 13 号　茅盾故居　　　35
东堂子胡同 75 号　蔡元培故居　　　36
细管胡同 9 号　田汉故居　　　　　　37
府学胡同 63 号　文天祥祠　　　　　38
西裱褙胡同 23 号　于谦祠　　　　　39
铁营胡同 10 号　徐世昌祠　　　　　40
帽儿胡同 37 号　婉容故居　　　　　41
黑芝麻胡同 13 号　奎俊府　　　　　42
东四四条 5 号　绵宜宅　　　　　　　43
朝阳门内大街 137 号　孚郡王府　　　44
东四六条 63 号　崇礼住宅　　　　　45
炒豆胡同 75 号　僧王府(之一)　　　46

炒豆胡同63号　僧王府（之二）　47
丰富胡同19号　老舍故居　48
西城区
小杨家胡同8号　老舍故居　49
后海北沿46号　宋庆龄故居　50
棉花胡同66号　蔡锷故居　51
西四北三条39号　程砚秋故居　52
护国寺街9号　梅兰芳故居　53
跨车胡同15号　齐白石故居　54
崇文区
草厂七条12号　广东惠州会馆　55
薛家湾胡同39号　钱氏宗祠　56
宣武区
南半截胡同7号　鲁迅故居绍兴会馆　57
米市胡同43号　康有为故居南海会馆　58
北半截胡同41号　谭嗣同故居济阳会馆　59
校场胡同三条2号　杨椒山故居　60
达智桥胡同12号　杨椒山祠　61
山西街甲13号　荀慧生故居　62
金井胡同1号　沈家本故居　63
珠朝街5号　中山会馆　64

三　佛塔、寺庙、道观、教堂　65
东城区
朝阳门内大街223号　大慈延福宫旧址　67
禄米仓胡同5号　智化寺　68
禄米仓胡同　智化寺万佛阁　69

西城区
砖塔胡同　万松老人塔　70
砖塔胡同68号　关帝庙旧址　71
烟袋斜街37号　广福观旧址　72
白塔寺东夹道　白塔寺　73
大石桥胡同61号　拈花寺旧址　74
正觉胡同甲9号　正觉寺旧址　75
象牙胡同与天主教堂　76
前细瓦厂胡同17号　"莲花山下院"旧址　77
崇文区
法华寺街65号　法华寺旧址　78
宣武区
法源寺前街　法源寺　79
扬威胡同9号　清真寺旧址　80

四　文化景观、历史建筑　81
东城区
国子监街　牌楼　83
铃铛胡同　钟楼　84
炮局头条　监狱旧址　85
西城区
地安门外大街　后门桥　86
银锭桥胡同　银锭桥　87
前海北沿18号　会贤堂旧址　88
兴华胡同13号　辅仁大学校友会　89
崇文区
西打磨厂街218号　医院旧址　90

魏染胡同 30 号《京报》馆旧址 91

五　四合院宅门　93
东城区
干面胡同 49 号——广亮大门　95
细管胡同 11 号——金柱大门　96
秦老胡同 35 号——如意门　97
东棉花胡同 15 号——砖雕拱门　98
官书院胡同 7 号——蛮子门　99
焕新胡同 21 号——蛮子门　100
慈慧胡同 9 号——广亮大门　101
前鼓楼苑胡同 7 号——蛮子门　102
飞龙桥胡同 5 号——蛮子门　103
盛芳胡同 1 号——如意门　104
北总布胡同 2 号——重檐牌楼门　105
黄米胡同 9 号——"半亩园"　106
大佛寺东街 2 号——广亮大门　107
汪芝麻胡同 53 号——如意门　108
什锦花园胡同 19 号——广亮大门　109
东四八条 61 号——蛮子门　110
板厂胡同 27 号——广亮大门　111
前永康胡同 7 号——广亮大门　112
西城区
庆丰胡同 13 号——金柱大门　113
千竿胡同 5 号——蛮子门　114
敬胜胡同 14 号——金柱大门　115
铜铁厂胡同 6 号——金柱大门　116

西斜街 42 号——垂花门　117
东福寿里 3 号——如意门　118
地安门内大街 35 号——西洋门　119
文华胡同 17 号——蛮子门　120
西单手帕胡同 12 号——蛮子门　121
宝产胡同 25 号——广亮大门　122
新街口头条 8 号——金柱大门　123
后公用胡同 8 号——如意门　124
正觉胡同 5 号——如意门　125
前细瓦厂胡同 11 号——广亮大门　126
崇文区
草厂横胡同 33 号——如意门　127
南芦草园胡同 12 号——金柱大门　128
长巷二条 2 号——如意门　129
宣武区
前孙公园胡同 1 号——如意门　130

六　胡同民居　131
东城区
后鼓楼苑胡同　133
白米仓胡同　134
火药局胡同　135
大经厂胡同　136
协和胡同　137
石雀胡同　138
顶银胡同　139
景阳胡同（之一）　140

景阳胡同（之二）	141
福祥胡同	142
大菊胡同	143
西城区	
南官房胡同	144
小金丝胡同	145
北官房胡同	146
南玉带胡同	147
前公用胡同	148
宫门口头条	149
后帽胡同	150
北海北夹道	151
大红罗厂南巷	152
小拐棒胡同	153
后细瓦厂胡同	154
园宏胡同	155
崇文区	
大市胡同	156
西厅胡同	157
薛家湾胡同	158
西八角胡同	159
南翔凤胡同	160
草厂二条	161
草厂四条（之一）	162
草厂四条（之二）	163
草厂五条	164
草厂七条	165
草厂八条	166
草厂九条	167
草厂十条	168
群智巷	169
清华街	170
得丰东巷	171
銮庆胡同	172
小席胡同	173
宣武区	
东北园北巷	174
百合园胡同	175
达智桥胡同	176
铁门胡同	177
校场小五条	178
培英胡同	179
梁家园东胡同	180
前孙公园西夹道	181
取灯胡同	182
红线胡同	183
粉房琉璃街	184
兴胜胡同	185
北大吉巷（之一）	186
北大吉巷（之二）	187
排子胡同	188
掌扇胡同	189
七井胡同	190
广安后巷	191
南大吉巷	192
贾家胡同	193
保安寺街	194
胡同写生日记选编	195

Contents

My Life in the Hutongs   Dai Chengsong

I. Traditional Shops, Firms, Pawnshops, Banks   1

Dongcheng District
- No.3 and No.5, Menlou Hutong, the Site of Traditional Pawnshops   3
- No. 86, Dongsi Sitiao Hutong, the Site of Traditional Pawnshops   4

Chongwen District
- Xixinglongjie Street, the Traditional Commercial Street (I)   5
- Xixinglongjie Street, the Traditional Commercial Street (II)   6
- Xixinglongjie Street, the Traditional Commercial Street (III)   7
- Xianyukoujie Street, the Traditional Commercial Street (I)   8
- Xianyukoujie Street, the Traditional Commercial Street (II)   9
- Xianyukoujie Street, the Traditional Commercial Street (III)   10
- Nanxiaoshun Hutong, the Traditional Business Shop   11
- Xidamochangjie Street, the Traditional Commercial Street (I)   12
- Xidamochangjie Street, the Traditional Commercial Street (II)   13
- Dajiang Hutong, the Site of Traditional Shops   14
- Buxiangzi Hutong, the Site of Traditional Firms   15

Xuanwu District
- Langfang Toutiao Hutong, the Site of a Gold Shop   16
- Dashilar Street, the Traditional Commercial Street   17
- Langfang Ertiao Hutong, the Traditional Commercial Street (I)   18
- Langfang Ertiao Hutong, the Traditional Commercial Street (II)   19
- Xiao Chunshu Hutong, the Site of Traditional Shops   20
- Peizhi Hutong and Meishijie Street, the Original Site of Traditional Shops   21
- No.41, Jiaochangkou Hutong, the Site of Traditional Shops   22
- No.57, Jiaochangkou Hutong, the Site of Traditional Shops   23
- No.1, Zongshu Xiejie Street, the Site of Traditional Shops   24
- No.31, Yangmeizhu Xiejie Street, the Site of Traditional Shops   25
- Qianshi Hutong, the Site of Traditional Shops   26
- No.45, Zhujia Hutong, the Site of "Linchunlou" Whorehouse   27

No.9, Zhumao Hutong, the Site of "Jubao Teahouse" Whorehouse	28
No.25, Xiaoli Hutong, the Site of "Ruixianglou" Whorehouse	29

II. Residences of Celebrities, Guild Halls, Princely Palaces, Ancestral Shrines — 31

Dongcheng District

NO.15, Doufuchi Hutong, the Residence of Mao Zedong	33
No.71, Dongsi Batiao Hutong, the Residence of Ye Shengtao	34
No.13, Houyuanensi Hutong, the Residence of Mao Dun	35
No.75, Dongtangzi Hutong, the Residence of Cai Yuanpei	36
No.9, Xiguan Hutong, the Residence of Tian Han	37
No.63, Fuxue Hutong, the Shrine for Wen Tianxiang	38
No.23, Xibiaobei Hutong, the Shrine for Yu Qian	39
No.10, Tieying Hutong, the Shrine for Xu Shichang	40
No.37, Maoer Hutong, the Family Home of Wan Rong	41
No.13, Heizhima Hutong, the Residence of Kui Jun	42
No.5, Dongsi Sitiao Hutong, Mianyizhai Siheyuan Courtyard	43
No.137, Chaoyangmenneidajie Street, Fuwangfu	44
No.63, Dongsi Liutiao Hutong, the Residence of Chongli (a royal scholar during Qing Emperor Guangxu's region)	45
No. 75, Chaodou Hutong, the Residence of Prince Zenggelinqin (I)	46
No. 63, Chaodou Hutong, the Residence of Prince Zenggelinqin (II)	47
No. 19, Fengfu Hutong, the Residence of Famous Writer Lao She	48

Xicheng District

No. 8, Xiaoyangjia Hutong, the Residence of Famous Writer Lao She	49
No. 46, Houhai Beiyan Street, the Residence of Soong Ching Ling	50
No. 66, Mianhua Hutong, the Residence of Cai E	51
No. 39, Xisi Beisantiao Hutong, the Residence of Cheng Yanqiu	52
No. 9, Huguosijie Street, the Residence of Mei Lanfang	53
No. 15, Kuache Hutong, the Residence of Qi Baishi	54

Chongwen District

No. 12, Caochang Qitiao Hutong, the Guild Hall of Huizhou	55
No. 39, Xuejiawan Hutong, the Qian Family's Ancestral Hall	56

Xuanwu District

No. 7, Nanbanjie Hutong, the Residence of Lu Xun, the Guild Hall of Shaoxing	57
No. 43, Mishi Hutong, the Residence of Kang Youwei, the Nanhai Guild Hall	58
No. 41, Beibanjie Hutong, the Residence of Tang Sitong, the Jiyang Guild Hall	59
No. 2, Jiaochang Hutong Santiao, the Residence of Yang Jiaoshan	60
No. 12, Dazhiqiao Hutong, the Shrine of Yang Jiaoshan	61

No. 13A, Shanxijie Street, the Residence of Xun Huisheng	62
No.1, Jingjin Hutong, the Residence of Shen Jiaben	63
No.5, Zhuchaojie Street, the Zhongshan Guild Hall	64

III. Pagodas, Temples, Churches — 65

Dongcheng District

No. 223, Chaoyangmennei Street, a Taoist Temple Originally Built in Ming Dynasty	67
No.5, Lumicang Hutong, Zhihuasi Buddhist Temple	68
Lumicang Hutong, Palace of Ten Thousand Buddhas at Zhihuasi Buddhist Temple	69

Xicheng District

Zhuanta Hutong, the Wansonglaoren Pagoda	70
No. 68, Zhuanta Hutong, the Site of the Guandimiao (War God) Temple	71
No. 37, Yandai ("Tobacco Pouch") Xiejie Street, the Site of Guangfuguan Taoist Temple	72
Baitasi Dongjiadao Hutong, the Baitasi Buddhist Temple	73
No.61, Dashiqiao Hutong, the Site of Nianhuasi Buddhist Temple	74
No. 9A, Zhengjue Hutong, the Site of Zhengjuesi Buddhist Temple	75
Xiangya Hutong and the Catholic Church	76
No. 17, Qianxiwachang Hutong, the Site of the "Lianhuashan Xiayuan" Buddhist Temple	77

Chongwen District

No.65, Fahuasijie Street, the Site of Fahuasi Buddhist Temple	78

Xuanwu District

Fayuansi Qianjie Street, the Fayuansi Buddhist Temple	79
No. 9, Yangwei Hutong, the Site of the Mosque	80

IV. Historic Buildings and Structures — 81

Dongcheng District

Guozijian Street, Pailou	83
Lingdang Hutong, the Bell Tower	84
Paoju Toutiao, the Site of a Prison	85

Xicheng Distrcit

Di'anmenwai Street, Houmen Bridge	86
Yindingqiao Hutong, the Yinding Bridge ("Silver Ingot Bridge")	87
No.18, Qianhai Beiyan, the site of Huixiantang Restaurant	88
No.13, Xinghua Hutong, the Furen University Alumni Association Office	89

Chongwen District

No. 218, Xidamochang Street, the Site of a Hospital	90
No.30, Weiran Hutong, the Site of the Editorial Office of Jingbao Newspaper	91

V. Gates of Siheyuan Courtyards — 93

Dongcheng District
No. 49, Ganmian Hutong, the Guangliang Gate	95
No.11, Xiguan Hutong, the Jinzhu Gate	96
No. 35, Qinlao Hutong, the Ruyi Gate	97
No. 15, Dongmianhua Hutong, Carved Brick Archway	98
No. 7, Guanshuyuan Hutong, the Manzimen Gate	99
No. 21, Huanxin Hutong, the Manzimen Gate	100
No. 9, Cihui Hutong, the Guangliang Gate	101
No. 7, Qiangulouyuan Hutong, the Manzimen Gate	102
No. 5, Feilongqiao Hutong, the Manzimen Gate	103
No. 1, Shengfang Hutong, the Ruyi Gate	104
No. 2, Beizongbu Hutong, the Double-eave, Pailou Style Courtyard Gate	105
No. 9, Mihuang Hutong, the Banmuyuan Private Garden	106
No. 2, Dafosi East Street, the Guangliang Gate	107
No.7, Wangzhima Hutong, the Ruyi gate	108
No.19, Shijinhuayuan Hutong, the Guangliang Gate	109
No. 61, Dongsibatiao Hutong, the Manzimen Gate	110
No. 27, Banchang Hutong, the Guangliang Gate	111
No. 7, Qianyongkang Hutong, the Guangliang Gate	112

Xicheng District
No. 13, Qingfeng Hutong, the Jinzhu Gate	113
No. 5, Qian'gan Hutong, the Manzimen Gate	114
No. 14, Jingsheng Hutong, the Jinzhu Gate	115
No. 6, Tongtiechang Hutong, the Jinzhu Gate	116
No. 42, Xixie Street, the Ornamental Inner Gate	117
No. 3, Dongfushouli, the Ruyi Gate	118
No. 35, Di'anmennei Street, the Western Style Arch	119
No. 17, Wenhua Hutong, the Manzimen Gate	120
No. 12, Shoupa Hutong, the Manzimen Gate	121
No. 25, Baochan Hutong, the Guangliang Gate	122
No. 8, Xinjiekou Toutiao Hutong, the Jinzhu Gate	123
No. 8, Hougongyong Hutong, the Ruyi Gate	124
No. 5, Zhengjue Hutong, the Ruyi Gate	125
No. 11, Qianxiwachang Hutong, the Guangliang Gate	126

Chongwen Distrcit
No. 33, Caochangheng Hutong, the Ruyi Gate	127
No. 12, Nanlucaoyuan Hutong, the Jinzhu Gate	128

No. 2, Changxiang Ertiao Hutong, the Ruyi Gate   129
Xuanwu District
No. 1, Qiansungongyuan Hutong, the Ruyi Gate   130

VI. Hutong Street Scenes   131

Dongcheng District
Hougulouyuan Hutong	133
Baimicang Hutong	134
Huoyaoju Hutong	135
Dajingchang Hutong	136
Xiehe Hutong	137
Shique Hutong	138
Dingyin Hutong	139
Jingyang Hutong (I)	140
Jingyang Hutong (II)	141
Fuxiang Hutong	142
Daju Hutong	143

Xicheng District
Nanguanfang Hutong	144
Xiaojinsi Hutong	145
Beiguanfang Hutong	146
Nanyudai Hutong	147
Qiangongyong Hutong	148
Gongmenkou Toutiao	149
Houmao Hutong	150
Beihai Beijiadao	151
Dahongluochang Nanxiang	152
Xiaoguaibang Hutong	153
Houxiwachang Hutong	154
Yuanhong Hutong	155

Chongwen District
Dashi Hutong	156
Xiting Hutong	157
Xuejiawan Hutong	158
Xibajiao Hutong	159
Nanxiangfeng Hutong	160
Caochang Ertiao Hutong	161
Caochang Sitiao Hutong (I)	162

Caochang Sitiao Hutong (II)	163
Caochang Wutiao Hutong	164
Caochang Qitiao Hutong	165
Caochang Batiao Hutong	166
Caochang Jiutiao Hutong	167
Caochang Shitiao Hutong	168
Qunzhi Lane	169
Qinghuajie Street	170
Defeng Dongxiang	171
Luanqing Hutong	172
Xiaoxi Hutong	173

Xuanwu District

Dongbeiyuan Beixiang	174
Baiheyuan Hutong	175
Dazhiqiao Hutong	176
Tiemen Hutong	177
Jiaochang Xiaowutiao	178
Peiying Hutong	179
Liangjiayuandong Hutong	180
Qiansungongyuan Jiadao	181
Qudeng Hutong	182
Hongxian Hutong	183
Fenfangliuli Street	184
Xingsheng Hutong	185
Beidajixiang Lane (I)	186
Beidajixiang Lane (II)	187
Paizi Hutong	188
Zhangshan Hutong	189
Qijing Hutong	190
Guang'an Houxiang	191
Nandajixiang	192
Jiajia Hutong	193
Baoansi Street	194

Selected Diaries on Hutong Sketching (In Chinese Only)   195

胡 同 缘
（序）

我生在北京，打小儿就与胡同有缘，曾住在东城根儿西侧的禄米仓东巷（旧为陆家大院），在大院里长大，胡同伴我走过了30个春秋，对大院和胡同的记忆既亲切又难忘。

我家住的院落，是有四五户人家的普通大院，没有气派的大门，没有迎门影壁，只有两扇漆皮剥落的木门，宽敞的院子里有三棵百年的大枣树和一棵合欢（马缨花）树。

走出院门，是整洁而幽静的胡同。出巷东口，穿东八宝胡同，经武学胡同，过智化寺山门，往东是小牌坊胡同，再往东就是东城根儿荒凉的残城墙和护城河了。我家院子西边是南北延伸的仓墙，老墙斑驳。巷北是仓后身儿，有条很窄的小巷可通大方家胡同，再往北是芳嘉园胡同、新鲜胡同和竹竿胡同。巷南是禄米仓胡同，再往南是大雅宝胡同、赵堂子胡同、赵家楼胡同等。禄米仓胡同西口是朝内南小街，对面是干面胡同，干面胡同以北依次是史家胡同、内务部街、演乐胡同、礼士胡同，以南依次是东堂子胡同、外交部街、西总布胡同等。这些熟悉的胡同，留下了我童年、少年和成年的身影，也留下了我过去美好的回忆。

我童年和少年时代经常去的地方是姥姥家——崇文区得丰东巷（旧为十间楼）。记忆中那是一个标准的四合院，高台阶，黑漆门，门口两边是一对精美的抱鼓石，门道里两条大条凳列放左右，砖雕影壁迎门，院中青砖墁地，北屋前有廊子，院里还养着金鱼，种着金银藤和石榴等植物。

走出院门，是曲折相连的胡同，北可去兴隆街，东可去草厂胡同，西通前门，南到三里河大街，这里的胡同也同样留下了我童年和少年时的美好回忆。

1995年，我家从禄米仓的平房搬到潘家园的楼房，虽然渐渐地远离了胡同的生活，然而与之相关的胡同情结，随着岁月的流逝，越发得深刻，越发得难忘了。——儿时在胡同里一起长大的伙伴，春季院里粉红色的马缨花散发的芳香，夏季枣树覆盖整个院儿的树荫和雨中屋檐下串串雨滴溅起的水泡儿，秋季打枣儿时枣儿落到地上和房上的声声作响，冬季雪后胡同里、屋顶上、树枝上的厚厚积雪……这些记忆碎片，常常引起我对美好往事的回想，如同陈酿那缕诱人的清香，弥漫在心，让人久久回味。

2000年，我开始步行上下班，每天趔行于潘家园与琉璃厂之间，一路上穿大街走小巷，要经过许多条胡同，走在胡同里，常常会触景生情，特别是我童年曾居住过、经常走过的胡同，如同又回到过去，倍感亲切。为了体会不同胡同的特点，我还经常改变线路，即使绕远也愿多走，走得多了，渐渐地发现一些胡同开始拆了，还有的墙上画着圈写着"拆"字，如同被判了死刑的"囚犯"。看到这些，心里有种无奈和凄凉。我也曾回去寻找过去的胡同，几年未见变化也很大，原有的马路被扩宽了，两边熟悉的建筑已无影无踪，取而代之的是一座座清一色没了个性的居民楼。站在原来熟悉的街道上，我却迷茫于不知置身何处，心中有种莫名的伤感，总想用某种方式把胡同留住，留下那些美好的记忆，我能够做些什么呢？

画画是我打小儿的爱好。记得小时候，经常在胡同的地上和墙上涂鸦。那时也不知道为什么，最喜欢的就是在胡同里画房子，这种爱好延续至今。

2002年我开始画速写，工作之余，我与几个同道的朋友经常到郊区的山里去写生，画农家小院。密云、怀柔、石景山等京郊大地的山山水水留下了我写生的足迹，也为我后来的胡同写生打下了基础。

2004年，命运多舛，由于种种原因，我不能经常出去写生了，但又不想丢下。一次与朋友聊天，朋友说："你不如以后改画胡同吧。"我听后觉得是个好点子，可以用绘画去实现留住胡同的心愿了，我很兴奋，开始尝试着在胡同里写生。但一开始没有胡同写生的经验，也不了解胡同的历史，只是没有目标地东画一幅，西画一幅，有时找了半天，因看哪儿都不入画，最终也没画成。为了寻找画胡同的突破口，我来到了图书馆，先了解了四合院与胡同的历史，发现了众多蕴藏在胡同中的人文历史和文化古迹。我把它们找出来分了类，如：故居、会馆、宗祠、王府、宅邸、佛寺、道观、教堂、商号、店铺、当铺、钱庄、旧宅院、四合院、历史古迹和胡同民居等，写下地址，分出城区，在地图上标出，接下来就是到胡同去寻找和写生了。我首先从名人故居和熟悉的胡同画起。从那时起，我每天背着画具和相机，带上水和干粮，奔走在京城的大小胡同中，边画边拍照，同时寻找新的"目标"，就这样开始了漫长的胡同写生之路。

有了计划后，也并非一帆风顺，有时听说哪里要拆，就先赶到那儿去画，但因为拆得进度过快，有些地方仅晚来一步，等待我的就只剩一地瓦砾了，懊悔不已。还有的地方拆得所剩无几，赶到现场也只能见最后一面了，近于凭吊。

记得我在画西裱背胡同的"于谦祠"时，当时费了很多周折才找到地方，可是西裱背胡同已经不存在了，现场被拆得满目疮痍，砖石瓦砾满地，废墟中只有一幢老门和相连的残墙还屹立着，墙上有个石牌写着"于谦祠"三字，斑驳的老门边上一棵柳树在尘风中摇曳着。我在废墟中转了许久，无奈地坐在瓦砾堆中，打开速写本，工地的尘土不时被施工的车辆扬起，落在身上和速写本上，我在全身心地投入时，似乎身边的一切全都虚化了，只有我与老宅的心灵对话。

在写生初期，对遇到的困难心理准备不足，有几次想放弃不画了，但又都顺利地闯了过来。

记得在画鲜鱼口和大栅栏这两条商业街之前，心里感觉不太可能画成，因为那里是人流如织，连站脚的地儿都难找到，更别说坐着画几个小时写生了。事先想如果到那里要是借不着椅子就彻底放弃不画了，让我没想到的是，无论是鲜鱼口路边开饭馆的老板，还是大栅栏东口看车的老太太，我一说，都非常热情地借给我椅子和凳子，尤其是大栅栏东口，人来人往，不能停，我见路口中间竖着一个"禁止车辆通行"的牌子，便在牌子后坐下，但凳子矮，视角低，构图不好，我又很为难地去麻烦老人，老人二话没说，到别处又帮我借了一个高椅子，因此我已经没有任何理由不画了。

另一次是去画康有为故居，我找到故居，见门前是一字影壁，正挡着大门，两边是出入口，地面还是下坡的。我在门前徘徊了许久，也没找到一个好的角度，正踌躇不前，想要放弃，天下起了小雨，我只好先到旁边的棚子下避雨，棚子下还有一把椅子，我坐下一看，正好从侧面看到故居的大门。我欣喜不已，就在棚子下边避雨边写生，冥冥中好像这场雨是为挽留我而下的，等我画好后雨也停了。我感谢那场及时雨，如果不是那场雨，可能也不会画到今天了。

我闯过了经验不足和心理不定阶段后，对画胡同有了一些经验，也有了信心，但更难熬的还有夏季的酷热、秋季的蚊咬和冬季的寒冷。

夏季的酷热最难熬，有时连个有树荫的地方也难找到。记得在画宣武区的"莲花山下院"时，正赶上最热的夏季，我从上午画到中午也没休息，正午的太阳直晒到地上几乎没有阴凉，胡同里的人也渐渐地少了，静静的只能听到笔触声，从墙上反射的光烤到我的脸上和胳膊上，半天下来通红。

到了秋季，被蚊虫叮咬是常事，尤其是那些不卫生的环境，有时为了画面构图的需要，不得不坐在挨着沟眼、下水道、厕所等泛味儿的地方。记得在画东城区盛芳胡同时，正是秋季，我画的门楼对面是个废品堆放地，又脏又味儿，雨后地面的积水满是蚊子，我画之前还是有备而来，先抹好"蚊不叮"，刚开始还好，但时间一长，我画得投入时，蚊子还是照叮。

冬季写生，时间长了手脚冻得不听使唤，手有时在不自然地抖。记得在画大吉巷时，天气很冷，正赶上这里要拆迁，有些居民已经搬走，为了赶在拆之前画完，我只好坚持着画，为了保暖，多画些时间，身上穿了七层衣服、八层裤子，我经常自嘲地说，我冬天画胡同，穿的是"七上八下"。但是，坐久了还是冷。

有了这些身心的历练，我的画面也开始成熟起来，逐渐找到了画胡同的感觉，从开始只画门楼向胡同转变，从速写向素描过渡。为了深入刻画，也需要更长的时间，从开始一天画一幅，到后来一周画一幅，虽然这样写生很辛苦，但我也乐在其中。

有路人问我为什么不拍照片回家画，我觉得在家画没有感觉，要深入刻画，照片无法像实物那样清楚。我在胡同写生时也拍了大量的照片，但我更想用画笔把胡同里最美最真的记忆留住，这就需要"修复"与"删减"。比如有些胡同正在拆迁，墙上被拆了个大洞，满地脏土垃圾，我都可以在画面里进行"修复"，以恢复胡同里的本来面目。同时为了追求纪实性，除了删去那些不入画的瑕疵以外，我画的胡同都尽可能地保持原貌。只有忠实于原貌的写生，才能还原老北京，证明老北京。

我在胡同写生还有更重要的原因，那就是用我亲身经历去感受老北京胡同的原生态。走进胡同，寻找着蕴藏的人文古迹，画着百年的历史风貌，听着熟悉的京腔京味，还有走街串巷的叫卖吆喝声。偶然掠过的鸽哨声，偶尔磨刀匠人清脆响亮的"惊闺"声，这些已与胡同融为了一体，是浓郁的胡同风情。我在胡同写生时还经常能听到一些传说故事，尽管有些可能是道听途说，也无从考证，但我每次把听到和看到的都记录下来，聊以自娱。

这些年我在胡同中寻找着、记录着，我走过的胡同已记不清，有些胡同已走过上千次，但还是乐此不疲。真是天道酬勤，这本画册记录了我从2004年到2007年这四年的胡同写生足迹，从所画的200多幅写生中选出不同种类、不同风格的作品180幅。写生水平有限，也没有多少得意之作，但敝帚自珍，因为每一幅画都凝聚着我对老北京胡同的爱心。随写生还附带简要文字介绍和部分日记，这些文字既非写作更非作品，只是我在胡同写生的记录，文字内容错误之处在所难免，尚祈读者不吝赐教。

我在胡同写生使用的是一次性绘图笔，它具有钢笔画线条清晰、不易涂改的特性，也有铅笔画层次丰富、栩栩如生的视觉效果，在这里仅为同道提供参考。

画册的出版得到了民间胡同保护者、胡同画家郑希成老先生的提携与首肯，得到了学苑出版社社长孟白先生的支持，编辑张翔与校对袁大威两位老师做了精心的编缀与校正，在此向上述先生深表诚挚的谢意。

在这里我还要感谢那些在胡同里曾经给我送过水、送过伞、指过路、扇过蚊子、借给我椅子、提供过有用信息、讲过胡同历史以及提过建议和鼓励过我的好心人，是他们给了我莫大的帮助。我想最好的感谢是我将继续地画下去，用笔把老北京的胡同留住，献给所有热爱老北京的人们。

愿北京胡同保存得长长久久，也愿我与胡同的缘相伴到永远！

戴程松

2010年9月19日

My Life in the Hutongs

Born in Beijing, I have lived a hutong-style life over the past three decades at Lumicang Hutong in Beijing's Dongcheng District. I can recall many stories from my childhood, boyhood and youth in the hutongs.

These memories of the hutongs nearby are both familiar and unforgettable: from my home, going eastward though Babao Hutong to Wuxue Hutong, and further to Xiaopaifang Hutong; going westward to Chaonei Xiaojie Street, and crossing the road to Pingmian Hutong, where Dafangjia Hutong and Xinxian Hutong lie in the north while Dayabao Hutong and Xiaoyabao Hutong lie in the south.

I started making sketch drawings in the year 2002. In my spare time then, I would often go with friends to suburban Beijing to make sketches of courtyards in the countryside. I have left my footprints all over Miyun, Huairou, Shijingshan and other suburban districts near Beijing. I believe these sketches actually paved the way for my hutong sketches.

After 2004, I had fewer chances to travel to the mountains to sketch, but I never quit sketch drawing.

One time, a friend of mine said to me, "Why not change to sketching the hutongs?" It struck me immediately that this could save both time and money, and most importantly, help to continue my dream. So I went and bought sketching paper and pens, and started to draw the hutongs.

As a matter of fact, I was a total rookie then and did not know the first thing about hutongs. So I turned to the library for an induction.

First, I would identify the name and location of all the places to be drawn, and categorize them as residences of celebrities, guild halls, ancestral halls, shops, temples, historical structures, princely mansions and siheyuan courtyards, etc. Places already drawn I would mark on the map.

Then I started with the hutongs and residences of celebrities that I was familiar with. For the residences, the drawings usually focus on the gate tower which is characteristic and impressive. From then on, I began my on-site investigations and operations throughout hutongs, large and small, to get them sketched.

At the same time, I also marked some interesting places that I came across accidentally, and hurried to sketch those that were to be demolished soon. In this way, I successfully took my first steps as planned.

Some passers-by asked me why I did not take photos and make the sketches at home. I think it is not the same thing, because it is hard for me to get the right feeling at home and photos cannot convey as much information as clearly as the real thing.

Another reason is that it was not convenient to take photos due to all the vehicles parked inside the hutongs. It would usually take several days to finish a sketch, with or without the autos. For places to be demolished, in order to convey the original look of the hutongs, I had to "restore" the scene which had been affected by holes on the wall or dirt on the ground.

One more major reason for me to sketch hutongs on site is that I prefer to observe, hear, and write down the stories and my feelings about Beijing, alone, by myself. It is most important to record the century-old traces, to hear the daily chatter over errands within the neighborhood, to record the vendors peddling along the hutongs, and to collect as many stories inside the hutongs as possible. Each sketch tells a unique story, which may have been unidentified hearsay, but I recorded them all very carefully just for fun.

Over these years, I have continued my searching and recording along the countless hutongs. Some places I have been to over forty times. This album has collected some hutong sketch drawings which were completed from 2004 to 2007, selected from over two hundred pieces of varied type and style.

Though the drawings are not that remarkable in artistic value, I cherish them all, as each one embodies part of my loving passion for the hutongs. Any comments or suggestions from you on this album is warmly welcome!

Finally, my gratitude goes to those kind-hearted people in the hutongs who offered me water, or an umbrella, or chairs and fans, who told me locations and the history of the hutongs, and who encouraged me to persist. It is these people that have given me the confidence to carry on. I believe my best response to their kind offerings is to keep going, so as to reward all the people who have helped and supported me.

Dai Chengsong

说　明

2010年7月1日，经国务院批准，北京市宣布撤销原宣武区、崇文区，分别并入西城区与东城区。现在沿着北京古老的中轴线的东西两侧分属，东城区与崇文区合并成立新的东城区，西城区与宣武区合并成立新的西城区。

老北京旧城的核心地带（东城、西城、宣武、崇文）四大城区，勾勒出明清北京城"凸"字形城廓。本书所收画作大多于并区之前完成，且为介绍老北京老旧胡同，故沿用旧的东城、西城、宣武、崇文四区名称规列，特此说明。

Introduction

On July 1, 2010, with the approval of the State Council, the Municipal Government of Beijing abolished the administrative Districts of Xuanwu and Chongwen, which were meiged with Xicheng and Dongcheng respectively.

The central axis of the city is ancient and grand, going from Yongdingmen Gate, along the Qianmendajie Street, across Zhengyangmen Gate and Tian'anmen Gate, through the golden glazed tiles of the Forbidden City, and finally out of the Deshengmen Gate. Now the eastern and western sides along the central axis have been adjusted, with Dongcheng District and Chongwen District merged as the new Dongcheng District, Xicheng District and Xuanwu District as the new Xicheng District.

The core area of old downtown Beijing (Dongcheng, Xicheng, Xuanwu, Chongwen) formerly known as the four districts, is convex-shaped, an outline of the Beijing city in Qing Dynasty and Ming Dynasty times. This book mainly focuses on the dated Hutong (lanes) in Beijing. So in the book, all the names of the former four districts, the core area of old downtown Beijing, remain according to the historical convention, for the convenience of the readers .

   Glossary-common types of gate

Ruiyi Gate (如意门): a small double door is set at the front of the gate house.

Manzi "Barbarians" Gate (蛮子门): a wide double door is set at the front part of the gate house.

Jinzhu Gate(金柱门): a wide double door is set in the center of the gate house.

Guangliang Gate (广亮门): a wide double door is set at the back of the gate house.

Chuihuamen / Festoon Gate (垂花门): usually the door linking the forecourt wiht the main courtyard, this kind of gate has two bits of wood sticking down in front, carved and painted like flower buds.

一、老店铺旧址
I. Traditional Shops, Firms, Pawnshops, Banks

2005年5月28日

门楼胡同3号、5号 老当铺旧址

门楼胡同位于东城区东北部，东起东直门南小街，西至横街，3号和5号曾是家当铺，门框是青石，设有铁门，大门上至今还嵌有石匾，上刻"泰和别馆"四字。此当铺是清代李氏所开。

No.3 and No.5, Menlou Hutong, the Site of Traditional Pawnshops

Menlou Hutong is located in the northeastern part of Dongcheng District, Beijing, starting from Dongzhimen Nanxiaojie Street westwards to the Hengjie Street. No. 3 and No. 5 along the Hutong were once used as pawnbroker's shops with four Chinese characters "Tai He Bie Guan" inscribed on the horizontal board on top of the gate.

2005年5月29日

东四四条86号　老店铺旧址

　　东四四条位于东城区东部，东起朝阳门北小街，西至东四北大街。画中是胡同西口86号，为民国时期的老式铺面建筑，铺面为二层小楼，一层明间辟为街门以供营业，二楼明间设阳台。

No. 86, Dongsi Sitiao Hutong, the Site of Traditional Pawnshops
Dongsi Sitiao Hutong is located in the eastern part of Dongcheng District, Beijing, starting from Chaoyangmen Beixiaojie Street in the east. No. 86 at the west entrance of the Hutong in the sketch drawing is in the traditional style for shops during the Republican period (1912-1949).

2004年8月29日

西兴隆街 老商街（之一）

西兴隆街位于崇文区北部，东起东兴隆街，西至鲜鱼口街，因兴隆寺而得名。街道两旁多有老式商店铺面，画中是西兴隆街西段，现已不存。

Xixinglongjie Street, the Traditional Commercial Street (I)

Xixinglongjie Street lies in the northern part of Chongwen District, Beijing, stretching from Dongxinglongjie Street in the east to Xianyukoujie Street in the west. On both sides of the street there are a few traditional style shops.

2004 年 10 月 4 日

西兴隆街　老商街（之二）

　　画中是西兴隆街中段。老北京最早的纸庄——敬记纸庄就在西兴隆街中段路北，开业于光绪二十四年。纸庄相对纸铺而言，它卖的是洋纸。随着岁月的流逝，这家纸庄早已无迹可寻，画中建筑也已不存。

Xixinglongjie Street, the Traditional Commercial Street (II)
The sketch drawing gives a view of the middle section of Xixinglongjie Street. "Jing's Paper Shop", the earliest paper shop to sell western-style paper in Beijing lay right on the north side at the middle part of Xixinglongjie Street.

2004 年 10 月 19 日

西兴隆街 老商街（之三）

　　画中是西兴隆街东段。过去这里是著名的商业街，是从崇文门外大街通往前门大街的重要通道。街两边多为二层中式砖木结构小楼，虽经风雨冲刷，但墙上的砖雕画依然精彩可见。因扩建，现街北侧房子已拆。

Xixinglongjie Street, the Traditional Commercial Street (III)

The sketch drawing gives a view of the middle section of Xixinglongjie Street. It was once a bustling commercial street, and now houses on the north side of the street have been demolished.

2004 年 8 月 30 日

鲜鱼口街　老商街（之一）

鲜鱼口街位于崇文区西北部，东起长巷五条，西至前门大街，因鱼市而得名。旧时附近的渔民在前门东南的泄水河（三里河）打鱼，再运到这里来卖，清代以后称鲜鱼口。鲜鱼口街是崇文区一条重要的胡同，曾有诸多的老字号如便宜坊、天兴居、祥聚公等，反映出浓厚的商贸文化，现已拆建。

Xianyukoujie Street, the Traditional Commercial Street (I)

Xianyukoujie Street lies in the northwestern part of Chongwen District, Beijing, starting from Changxiang Wutiao Hutong in the east. The street gets its name (literally "fresh fish intersection") from a fish market along the street in the past. It is regarded as an important hutong of Chongwen District.

2004年8月30日

鲜鱼口街 老商街（之二）

　　清代鲜鱼口街曾失火，烧了半条街。传说在着火的前一天，一个老头挂着竹篮卖麻酱烧饼和咸鱼，口中喊"咸（鲜）鱼大火烧"。此街在历史上是一条繁华街道，清代中后期，这里已发展成店铺相连的商业街了。现已拆建。

Xianyukoujie Street, the Traditional Commercial Street (II)

In the Qing Dynasty (1644-1911), there was a great fire in Xianyukoujie Street which damaged about half of the buildings. The street was a busy street in the past, but now it has been demolished for redevelopment.

{ 鲜鱼口街 老商街（之三）}

　　位于崇文区北部。画中是长巷三条与鲜鱼口街十字路口之间，路边多是旧式两层铺面店，多是租给外地人居住在此做小买卖，经营蔬菜、水果和日用百货等。现已拆建。

Xianyukoujie Street, the Traditional Commercial Street (III)

The sketch gives a view of the crossing between Changxiang Santiao Hutong and Xianyukoujie Street which lies in the northern part of Chongwen District, Beijing. Along the street there were once vegetable shops, fruits shops and grocery shops, but now the buildings have been demolished for redevelopment.

2004 年 9 月 1 日

南晓顺胡同　老商铺旧址

　　南晓顺胡同位于崇文区西北部，北起鲜鱼口街，南至大江胡同。明代时称此巷为"孝顺牌胡同"，原意为孝顺父母之人立的牌坊。此街旧时以工商业居多，多中等铺户和小作坊，画中是南晓顺胡同与得丰西巷相接处一老商铺门脸。

Nanxiaoshun Hutong, the Traditional Business Shop

Nanxiaoshun Hutong lies in the northwestern part of Chongwen District, Beijing, starting from Xianyukoujie Street in the north to Dajiang Hutong in the south. The street was once famous for many handicrafts and businesses and small workshops. The sketch gives a view of a traditional style shop at the crossing between Nanxiaoshun Hutong and Defengxixiang Hutong.

2004 年 10 月 22 日

2004 年 10 月 2 日

西打磨厂街　老店街（之一）

　　西打磨厂街位于崇文区西北部，东起东打磨厂街，西至前门大街，因有许多打磨铜器和石器的作坊而得名。此街商业发达，多旧式小店铺，现在还依稀保存了昔日风貌。

Xidamochangjie Street, the Traditional Commercial Street (I)
Xidamochangjie Street lies in the northwestern part of Chongwen District, Beijing, and got its name from a few workshops specialized in polishing bronze or stone utensils. ("damo" means to polish)

2004年10月3日

西打磨厂街　老店街（之二）

　　清末民初，西打磨厂是前门外四条著名商街之一，八大祥之一的瑞生祥、京城大饭庄之一的福寿堂，都曾在此红火过。大小不一的安寓客店，还有铁柱宫火神庙那些儒道杂陈的庙宇，以及京城最早的民信局，都鳞次栉比地挤在这里。

Xidamochangjie Street, the Traditional Commercial Street (II)

Xidamochangjie Street was once one of the four celebrated commercial streets near Qianmen in late Qing Dynasty (1644-1911) and early Republican period (1912-1949).

2006年8月17～26日

大江胡同 老商铺旧址

　　大江胡同位于崇文区西北部，东南起自珠市口东大街，西北至前门大街，以蒋姓谐音而来。画中为大江胡同西北口，这里曾经是繁华的商业街，也是通往前门大街的捷径。

Dajiang Hutong, the Site of Traditional Shops

Dajiang Hutong, lying in the northwestern part of Chongwen District, Beijing, was once a bustling commercial street.

布巷子胡同 老商号旧址

布巷子胡同位于崇文区西北部，北起鲜鱼口街，南至珠市口东大街。巷内多批发兼或零售布匹的店铺，故名布巷子。画中是胡同中间保留完好的中西结合式建筑"益记布庄"。

Buxiangzi Hutong, the Site of Traditional Firms

Buxiangzi Hutong, lying in the northwestern part of Chongwen District, Beijing, was once noted for its many wholesale or retail cloth shops.

2006年8月12～16日

2005年4月26~27日

廊坊头条　金店旧址

　　廊坊头条位于宣武区东北部，东起前门大街，西至煤市街。明代永乐年间所建，时称廊房胡同，以其巷两侧皆为廊式铺房之故。旧时钱庄、银号、珠宝店、首饰楼、玉器、制印、锦盒等店铺集聚此处。此画是一座西洋式的金店，现门面上还有"金店"二字。

Langfang Toutiao Hutong, the Site of a Gold Shop

Langfang Toutiao Hutong starting from Qianmen Street gets its name from the rows of passage-style shops on both sides of the street. In the sketch you can see a western style shop selling gold articles, even now the name "gold shop" is legible on top of the front door.

2004 年 9 月 4 日

大栅栏街　老商街

　　大栅栏街位于宣武区东北部，东起前门大街，西至煤市街。因东西胡同口各建有一座大栅栏，故而得名。大栅栏街是北京著名的商业街，店铺鳞次栉比，且著名老店铺多，如同仁堂药铺、瑞蚨祥绸布店、内联陞鞋店、张一元茶庄等。

Dashilar Street, the Traditional Commercial Street

Dashilar Street lies in the northeastern part of Xuanwu District, Beijing, and gets its name from the two big fences (pronounced "da zhalan" in Chinese and later changed to "Dashilar" in Beijing dialect) at the east and west entrances of the Hutong. Dashilar Street is one of the most famous commercial streets in Beijing, with rows of shops, including some time-honored brand-name shops.

廊坊二条　老商街（之一）

廊坊二条位于宣武区东北部，东起前门大街，西至煤市街。明代永乐年间所建，朝廷"召民居住，召商居货"，清乾隆年形成古玩、玉器、彩灯铺一条街，三盛兴、恒聚兴、聚丰厚、宝权号等现仍留古老风貌，但老店俱废，多为小饭馆代替。画中是二条西口。

Langfang Ertiao Hutong, the Traditional Commercial Street (I)

This hutong runs from Qianmen Street eastward to Meishijie Street. During Emperor Qianlong's reign (1736 - 1796) in Qing Dynasty, the Hutong gradually turned into a special street with shops dealing with antiques, jade articles and color lanterns. The sketch drawing shows its west entrance.

2004年9月12日

廊坊二条 老商街（之二）

位于宣武区东北部。历史上廊房二条以经营古玩、玉器著世，有"玉器古玩街"之称，至今还保留着清代的老店铺。这些砖木结构的二层小楼，建筑独特，楼下为商店，楼上是账房和主人休息之所。现仍能见到当年的风貌，但多为小饭馆代替。画中是二条东口。

Langfang Ertiao Hutong, the Traditional Commercial Street (II)

The Hutong lies in the northeastern part of Xuanwu District, Beijing. In the past, Langfang Ertiao was well known for antiques and jade business. The sketch shows its east entrance.

2004 年 9 月 15 日

2004 年 9 月 6 日

小椿树胡同　老店铺旧址

　　小椿树胡同位于宣武区东北部，东起煤市街，西至元兴夹道。煤市街从清代中期以后，从煤栈、煤商买卖的交易市场，逐渐地发展成各种店铺都有的商业街。画中是小椿树胡同东口与煤市街路西的老商铺旧址，现已不存。

Xiaochunshu Hutong, the Site of Traditional Shops

Xiaochunshu Hutong lies in the northeastern part of Xuanwu District, Beijing. In the mid-Qing Dynasty (1644-1911), it was a place for coal stores and coal merchants. The sketch shows an old shop which no longer exists along Meishijie Street.

2004年9月8日

{ 培智胡同　老店铺旧址 }

　　培智胡同位于宣武区东北部，东起煤市街，西至棕树二条。因其相邻的胡同称培英胡同，所以取名培智胡同。清代光绪年间胡同中有"小马神庙"，很小，只有一间房。画中是培智胡同东口与煤市街路西的二层老店铺旧址，现已不存。

Peizhi Hutong and Meishijie Street, the Site of Traditional Shops
Peizhi Hutong lies in the northeastern part of Xuanwu District, Beijing. The sketch shows a two-storey shop which no longer exists at the east entrance of Peizhi Hutong on the west side of Meishijie Street.

21

2004 年 9 月 28 日

校场口胡同 41 号　老店铺旧址

校场口胡同位于宣武门外大街，明代称将军教场，清代称将军校场。明清两朝这里是军队演武操练的场所，光绪末年废除科举与旧式弓箭比赛，校场逐渐形成居民区。画中是胡同 41 号老店铺，曾经是油盐粮店，现已成民居。

No.41, Jiaochangkou Hutong, the Site of Traditional Shops
Jiaochangkou Hutong lies along Xuanwumenwai Street, once used as a place for military training and drills during the Ming Dynasty (1368-1644) and Qing Dynasty (1644-1911) times, but later turned into a residential area.

2007年8月22～29日

校场口胡同57号 老店铺旧址

　　校场口胡同位于宣武区中北部，东起宣武门外大街，西至老墙根街，因明清两朝军队在此演武、操练而得名。画中是胡同57号的二层老店铺，现已成民居。

No.57, Jiaochangkou Hutong, the Site of Traditional Shops

Jiaochangkou Hutong lies in the central northern part of Xuanwu District. It was once well known as a place for military drills and training during the Ming Dynasty (1368-1644) and Qing Dynasty (1644-1911) times, but later turned into a residential area.

2005年7月13日

棕树斜街 1 号　老店铺旧址

　　棕树斜街位于宣武区东北部,东北起自大力胡同,西南止于石头胡同。清代时称王寡妇斜街,光绪年间谐音雅化为王广福斜街,1965年定名为棕树斜街。画中为二层旧式店铺,过去街上这样的店铺较多。

No.1, Zongshu Xiejie Street, the Site of Traditional Shops
Zongshu Xiejie Street starts from Dali Hutong in the northeast. The sketch shows a two-storey traditional style shop which was typical in old times.

| 杨梅竹斜街31号 |
| 老店铺旧址 |

    杨梅竹斜街位于宣武区东北部，东起煤市街，西至延寿街，清光绪年间，由"杨媒斜街"谐音为"杨梅竹斜街"。在民国期间此街是有名的文化街，当时有名的世界书局、开明书店、广益书局、环球书局、大东书局等设在这条街内。画中是胡同31号，即是当时的世界书局旧址，中式房屋加上西洋门脸儿。

No.31, Yangmeizhu Xiejie Street, the Site of Traditional Shops

Yangmeizhu Xiejie Street lies in the northeastern part of Xuanwu District. It was famous for culture during the Republican period (1912-1949). The sketch shows No. 31 inside the Hutong, which was once the office building of World Publishers.

2007年5月2～5日

2005年8月4～6日

钱市胡同 老钱庄旧址

钱市胡同位于宣武区东北部，东起前门外珠宝市街，西侧为死巷，是京城最窄的胡同之一。这条胡同总长50米、宽70厘米，这里曾是清末民初钱庄的集中之地，垄断着北京的白银与铜钱的兑换价格。路北建有三层灰色小楼，现还有几家住户。

Qianshi Hutong, the Site of Traditional Shops

Qianshi Hutong is a dead-end lane, said to be the narrowest Hutong in Beijing, on the west side of Zhubaoshi Street outside Qianmen. It was the location of many private banks during late Qing Dynasty (1644-1911) and early Republican period (1912-1949), controlling the exchange rate of silver and bronze coins in Beijing.

2004 年 9 月 11 日

朱家胡同 45 号 "临春楼" 妓院旧址

  朱家胡同位丁宣武区东北部，北起大栅栏西街，南至棕树斜街。因有朱姓大户在此居住，故得名。朱家胡同在清末民国时期，曾是有名的妓院集中区，有的院落门楼和墙上至今还残留有妓院的刻字号，临春楼即是其一。

No.45, Zhujia Hutong, the Site of "Linchunlou" Whorehouse
Zhujia Hutong lies in the northeastern part of Xuanwu District, Beijing. It was once an area for whorehouses. Some whorehouse names carved on walls are still legible.

2005年5月11～12日

朱茅胡同9号 "聚宝茶室" 妓院旧址

朱茅胡同位于宣武区东北部，北起大栅栏西街，南端往西至燕家胡同。旧时胡同居住几家收买猪毛猪鬃的商贩，俗称猪毛胡同，雅化为朱茅胡同。这条胡同在1949年前，有十几处妓院，是北京妓院聚集处之一，聚宝茶室即是其一。

No.9, Zhumao Hutong, the Site of "Jubao Teahouse" Whorehouse

Zhumao Hutong lies in the northeastern part of Xuanwu District, Beijing. It was one of the areas with around a dozen whorehouses before 1949.

28

2005 年 5 月 10 日

小力胡同 25 号 "蕊香楼"妓院旧址

　　小力胡同位于宣武区东北部,北起大栅栏西街,南至大力胡同,由小李纱帽胡同谐音而得名。在北京解放前,此处曾是妓院集聚地之一,它和青风巷、棕树斜街、朱茅胡同、百顺胡同、韩家胡同、石头胡同、陕西巷等合称"八大胡同",蕊香楼即是妓院其一。

No.25, Xiaoli Hutong, the Site of "Ruixianglou" Whorehouse
Xiaoli Hutong lies in the northeastern part of Xuanwu District, Beijing. It was one of the areas for whorehouses before the liberation of Beijing.

二、名人故居、会馆、王府、宗祠

II. Residences of Celebrities, Guild Halls,
Princely Palaces, Ancestral Shrines

2004年8月3日

豆腐池胡同 15 号 毛泽东故居

　　豆腐池胡同位于东城区西北部，东起宝钞胡同，西至旧鼓楼大街。明代时称豆腐陈胡同，疑是陈姓做豆腐者居此。豆腐池胡同西有宏恩观，明建，现尚有部分遗存。画中为胡同 15 号，是杨昌济（毛泽东岳父）故宅，民国七年（1918 年）毛泽东来京曾居于此。

NO.15, Doufuchi Hutong, the Residence of Mao Zedong

Doufuchi Hutong lies in the northwestern part of Dongcheng District, Beijing. Mao Zedong, former chairman of the People's Republic of China lived here in 1918.

2004年8月18日

| 东四八条71号　叶圣陶故居 |

　　东四八条位于东城区东部，东起朝阳门北小街，西至东四北大街。画中为胡同71号，原是清代为宫中掌管帘子的王姓官吏所盖，解放后为教育家叶圣陶故居。宅落三进，垂花门、影壁、游廊保存完好。院内典雅质朴，充满文人气息，叶圣陶寓此曾创作了《叶圣陶童话选》等。

No.71, Dongsi Batiao Hutong, the Residence of Ye Shengtao

Dongsi Batiao Hutong lies in the eastern part of Dongcheng District, Beijing. It was once the residence of educationist Ye Shengtao who wrote Selected Fairy Tales by Ye Shengtao and other famous books.

2004年8月14日

后圆恩寺胡同 13 号　茅盾故居

后圆恩寺胡同位于东城区西北部，东起交道口南大街，西至南锣鼓巷。元代时胡同里曾建有圆恩寺，现已不存。清称后圆恩寺胡同。画中为胡同 13 号，系茅盾先生的故居，故居内起居室、工作室、会客室一切陈设全为旧物，保留原貌。

No.13, Houyuanensi Hutong, the Residence of Mao Dun

Houyuanensi Hutong lies in the northwestern part of Dongcheng District, Beijing. The sketch shows courtyard No. 13 which was once the residence for famous Chinese writer Mao Dun.

2004年8月22日

> 东堂子胡同75号　蔡元培故居

　　东堂子胡同位于东城区东南部。东起朝阳门南小街，西至东单北大街，明代称堂子胡同。民国时，北大校长蔡元培曾居胡同75号。2000年末小院险些被拆，后经有关部门保护，又得以修复。

No.75, Dongtangzi Hutong, the Residence of Cai Yuanpei

Dongtangzi Hutong lies in the southeastern part of Dongcheng District, Beijing. During the Republican period (1912-1949), Cai Yuanpei, president of Peking University, lived in No. 75.

2004年8月28日

细管胡同9号 田汉故居

　　细管胡同位于东城区西北部，东起东四北大街，西至北剪子巷。此巷原有济阳卫仓，明代天启二年改为户部的宝泉局，又称钱法堂。民国时作细罐胡同。画中为胡同9号，是田汉故居。田汉是国歌《义勇军进行曲》的词作者。

No.9, Xiguan Hutong, the Residence of Tian Han
Xiguan Hutong lies in the northwestern part of Dongcheng District, Beijing. The sketch shows No. 9 courtyard inside the hutong which was once the residence for Tian Han who wrote the lyrics for the national anthem of the People's Republic of China.

府学胡同63号　文天祥祠

　　府学胡同位于东城区西北部，东起东四北大街，西至交道口南大街，因顺天府学而得名。画中为府学胡同的文天祥祠，祠堂里面有棵传为文天祥亲手所植的枣树，其中一条树枝一直指向南方，其寓意就是文天祥的著名诗篇《指南录》中的"臣心一片磁针石，不指南方不肯休"。

No.63, Fuxue Hutong, the Shrine for Wen Tianxiang

Fuxue Hutong lies in the northwestern part of Dongcheng District, Beijing, deriving its name ("Prefectural School") from its having been the location of the Shuntian prefectural School. The sketch shows the shrine for Wen Tianxiang, a loyal official of the Song Dynasty (960 - 1279) who was imprisoned here for 7 years during the Yuan Dynasty (1279 - 1368).

2004年8月28日

| 西裱褙胡同 23 号　于谦祠 |

西裱褙胡同位于东城区东南部,东起北京邮政通信枢纽西墙,西至崇文门内大街,因昔日巷内多从事裱褙者而得名。画中为胡同北侧 23 号的于谦祠,祠中曾塑于谦像。于谦是明代著名军事家、政治家。现胡同已不存,只留有于谦祠。

No.23, Xibiaobei Hutong, the Shrine for Yu Qian

Xibiaobei Hutong lies in the southeastern part of Dongcheng District, Beijing, getting its name from the tradition that many paperhangers lived in the lane. The sketch shows No. 23 on the northern side of the hutong, known as the Shrine of Yu Qian, a famous strategist and politician of the Ming Dynasty (1368-1644).

2004 年 8 月 24 日

2005年5月27日

铁营胡同10号　徐世昌祠

　　铁营胡同位于东城区东部，东起流水巷，西至东四五条，旧称铁箭营。民国初年总统徐世昌故居即在铁营胡同，现存一座两卷勾连搭和一座三卷勾连搭建筑，据说铁营胡同10号是徐世昌祠。

No.10, Tieying Hutong, the Shrine for Xu Shichang
Tieying Hutong lies in eastern part of Dongcheng District, Beijing. In early Republican period (1912-1949), the residence of president Xu Shichang was right inside Tieying Hutong.

2004 年 8 月 14 日

帽儿胡同 37 号　婉容故居

　　帽儿胡同位于东城区北部，东起南锣鼓巷，西至地安门外大街。明代称梓潼庙文昌宫，文昌宫位于胡同 21 号，清代称冒儿胡同。帽儿胡同旧迹颇多，9 号、11 号为可园，35 号、37 号为宣统皇后婉容娘家，婉容大婚之前居于此，俗称娘娘府。画中为 37 号垂花门。

No.37, Maoer Hutong, the Family Home of Wan Rong

Maoer Hutong lies in the northern part of Dongcheng District, Beijing. No. 35 and No. 37 was the family home of Wan Rong, who married last Qing Emperor Xuantong. Wan Rong lived there until her wedding, so the yard is traditionally called "Queen's Residence".

2004年8月15日

黑芝麻胡同13号 奎俊府

　　黑芝麻胡同位于东城区西北部，东起南锣鼓巷，西至南下洼子胡同，明代称何纸马胡同。此巷内有何姓人家开办一名"七巧斋"的糊纸马作坊，后谐音讹称黑芝麻。画中为胡同内13号，原是清代光绪年间的内务府大臣、兵部尚书奎俊的宅邸，广亮大门前有一对上马石，院内有影壁、垂花门和抄手游廊等。西为住宅，东为花园是北京著名的四合院。

No.13, Heizhima Hutong, the Residence of Kui Jun

Heizhima Hutong lies in the northwestern part of Dongcheng District, Beijing. Inside the hutong, there is a famous Siheyuan courtyard which was once the residence of Kui Jun, minister of internal affairs during Qing Emperor Guangxu's reign.

2004年8月24日

东四四条5号　绵宜宅

东四四条位于东城区东部，东起朝阳门北小街，西至东四北大街，明代称四条胡同。画中是胡同5号，为清代宗室绵宜宅，是典型的中型四合院。院落三进，垂花门、抄手游廊、后罩房一应俱全。

No.5, Dongsi Sitiao Hutong, Mianyizhai Siheyuan Courtyard

Dongsi Sitiao Hutong lies in the eastern part of Dongcheng District, Beijing. It was called Sitiao Hutong from the Ming Dynasty (1368-1644). Inside the hutong lies a typical medium sized Siheyuan courtyard.

2005 年 10 月 5 日

朝阳门内大街 137 号　孚郡王府

　　孚王府位于东城区东南部。在朝阳门内大街 137 号内，俗称九爷府，为清代道光皇帝的第九个儿子奕譓府邸，它的前身是怡亲王府，其现在府内中轴线建筑仍保存完好。画中为孚郡王府内大门，朱漆门扇上排列着纵九横七 63 颗门钉，门前矗立的石狮有两人多高，足见其当初营造时的宏大规模。

No.137, Chaoyangmenneidajie Street, Fuwangfu

Fuwangfu, conventionally called Ninth Prince's Palace, lies in the southeastern part of Dongcheng District, Beijing. Inside the compound, buildings along the central axis are well preserved.

2005年10月1日

东四六条63号 崇礼住宅

东四六条位于东城区东部，东起朝阳门北小街，西至东四北大街。六条胡同西口内63号和65号原为一组相连的大宅，为清代光绪年间大学士崇礼的住宅。崇礼字受之，姓姜氏，一般人皆以为蒋姓称蒋四爷。画中为63号广亮大门。

No.63, Dongsi Liutiao Hutong, the Residence of Chongli

Dongsi Liutiao Hutong lies in the eastern part of Dongcheng District, Beijing, and contains the residence of a great scholar during Qing Emperor Guangxu's reign. The sketch shows the wide and spacious entrance gate to No. 63 courtyard inside the hutong.

2006年6月2～4日

炒豆胡同 75 号　僧王府（之一）

炒豆胡同位于东城区西北部，东起交道口南大街，西至南锣鼓巷。胡同内 77 号和 75 号是清末僧格林沁府。僧格林沁府今天基本完好，只是析为几个部分。胡同内共有 5 个大门临街，画中为炒豆胡同 75 号，其大门石墩上的狮子有四层，雕工精美，寓意四世同堂。

No. 75, Chaodou Hutong, the Residence of Prince Senggelinqin (I)

Chaodou Hutong lies in the northwestern part of Dongcheng District, Beijing. No. 75 and No. 77 in the hutong were once the residence of Prince Senggelinqin in late Qing Dynasty (1644-1911).

2006 年 6 月 5 ～ 9 日

炒豆胡同 63 号 僧王府 （之二）

炒豆胡同位于东城区西北部，东起交道口南大街，西至南锣鼓巷。胡同 63 号和 65 号是清末僧格林沁府。僧格林沁府今天基本完好，只是析为几个部分。胡同内共有王府的五个大门临街，此画为 63 号王府大门。

No. 63, Chaodou Hutong, the Residence of Prince Senggelinqin (II)

Chaodou Hutong lies in the northwestern part of Dongcheng District, Beijing. No. 63 and No. 65 yards were once the residence of Prince Senggelinqin in late Qing Dynasty (1644-1911). The sketch shows the gate of No. 63, the royal residence, inside the hutong.

2004 年 8 月 21 日

丰富胡同 19 号　老舍故居

　　丰富胡同位于东城区西南部，北起大草场胡同，南至灯市口西街，胡同内 19 号是著名作家老舍先生故居。老舍夫人为其院落定名为"丹柿小院"，在这里老舍创作了《方珍珠》、《龙须沟》、《茶馆》等大批著作。

No. 19, Fengfu Hutong, the Residence of Famous Writer Lao She
Fengfu Hutong lies in the southwestern part of Dongcheng District, Beijing. No. 19 courtyard inside the hutong was once the residence for famous writer Lao She.

2004 年 8 月 20 日

小杨家胡同 8 号　老舍故居

　　小杨家胡同位于西城区东北部，西起新街口南大街，北至大杨家胡同，形状特殊，口小内大，犹如葫芦。清宣统元年称小羊圈。作家老舍于光绪二十五年出生在 8 号院，《四世同堂》就是他以这条胡同为背景，描写抗日战争时期北京人生活的作品。

No. 8, Xiaoyangjia Hutong, the Residence of Famous Writer Lao She

Xiaoyangjia Hutong lies in the northeastern part of Xicheng District, Beijing. Writer Lao She was born in No. 8 courtyard inside the hutong in 1900, the 25th year of Qing Emperor Guangxu's reign, and his famous novel Four Generations Under One Roof was based on life in the Xiaoyangjia Hutong.

2004 年 8 月 8 日

| 后海北沿 46 号　宋庆龄故居 |

　　后海北沿位于西城区北部，东起小石碑胡同，西至孝友胡同，有醇亲王府末代皇帝出生地（摄政王府）、大藏龙华寺与诗人田间故居。画中是 46 号，原为国家名誉主席宋庆龄故居。

No. 46, Houhai Beiyan Street, the Residence of Soong Ching Ling

Houhai Beiyan Street lies in the northern part of Xicheng District, Beijing, which was Prince Chun's Palace. China's last Emperor was born here. No. 46, once the gardens of the palace, was the residence of Soong Ching Ling, honorary chairman of the People's Republic of China.

2004年8月19日

棉花胡同66号　蔡锷故居

　　棉花胡同位于西城区东北部，北起罗儿胡同，南至护国寺街。棉花胡同66号为蔡锷故居。故居为二进院落，房屋由回廊相连，蔡锷曾在此居住两年。蔡锷字松坡，护国运动的领袖之一，因反对袁世凯复辟而彪炳史册。

No. 66, Mianhua Hutong, the Residence of Cai E
Mianhua Hutong lies in the northeastern part of Xicheng District, Beijing. No. 66 was once the residence for Cai E, who is remembered for his bravery against the Yuan Shi Kai, who tried to restore the monarchy.

2004年8月7日

西四北三条39号 程砚秋故居

　　西四北三条位于西城区中部，东起西四北大街，西至赵登禹路。画中为39号程砚秋故居。程砚秋是四大名旦之一，京戏程派艺术的创始人。故居为两进院落，前后由月亮门和垂花门相连，故居内陈设仍保持原状。

No. 39, Xisi Beisantiao Hutong, the Residence of Cheng Yanqiu

Xisi Beisantiao Hutong lies in the central part of Xicheng District, Beijing. The sketch shows No. 39, once the residence for Cheng Yanqiu, a man who played female roles in Beijing opera, founder of the Cheng School of Beijing Opera.

2004年9月18日

> 护国寺街9号　梅兰芳故居

　　护国寺街位于西城区东北部，街东起德胜门内大街，西至新街口南大街，胡同内因有护国寺而得名。其街北侧9号为梅兰芳故居。进门后影壁前是梅先生汉白玉半身像，进二门是正院，北房七间分别是客厅、书房、卧室及起居室，陈设依旧。东西厢房展示的是梅先生的遗作和穿过的戏衣剧照等，现为梅兰芳纪念馆。

No. 9, Huguosijie Street, the Residence of Mei Lanfang

Huguosijie Street lies in the northeastern part of Xicheng District, Beijing. No. 9 on the north side was once the residence and now the museum for Mei Lanfang, famous Beijing Opera master, a man who played female roles.

2004 年 8 月 25 日

跨车胡同 15 号　齐白石故居

　　跨车胡同位于西城区中部，南起辟才胡同，北端向西倾斜，通向太平桥大街，清代称车子胡同。画中为跨车胡同 15 号，是画家齐白石故居，故居是一座三合院带跨院的住宅，坐西朝东，白石老人在这里度过了 44 个春秋。现胡同已拆，只留故居。

No. 15, Kuache Hutong, the Residence of Qi Baishi

Kuache Hutong lies in the central part of Xicheng District, Beijing. The sketch shows No. 15, once the residence for Qi Baishi, famous Chinese traditional ink painter who spent nearly half a century there.

2005 年 6 月 5 日

草厂七条12号　广东惠州会馆

　　草厂七条位于崇文区西北部，北起西兴隆街，南至北芦草园胡同。胡同内曾有南安、袁州、惠州会馆。画中为草厂七条12号的广东惠州会馆旧址。门楼以红色砖材为主，属近现代门楼，拱券门和其他部位风格特征体现出中西结合的建筑风格。

No. 12, Caochang Qitiao Hutong, the Guild Hall of Huizhou

Caochang Qitiao Hutong lies in the northwestern part of Chongwen District, Beijing. The sketch shows No. 12 which was once the Guild Hall of Huizhou in southeast China's Guangdong Province.

薛家湾胡同39号　钱氏宗祠

　　薛家湾胡同位于崇文区西北部，东起北武圣巷，西至北桥湾街，原为旧三里河拐弯处。相传有一使船的人家姓薛，故名。画中是胡同内37号，即清末官宦家"钱氏宗祠"。"钱氏宗祠"三层院落，祠内原供有钱王像等历史文物，现已不存。

No. 39, Xuejiawan Hutong, the Qian Family's Ancestral Hall

Xuejiawan Hutong lies in the northwestern part of Chongwen District, Beijing. The sketch shows No. 37, the Qian Family's Ancestral Hall built in late Qing Dynasty.

2006年7月28～8月1日

南半截胡同 7 号　鲁迅故居绍兴会馆

南半截胡同位于宣武区中部，北起北半截胡同，南至南横西街，成名于明代，称半截胡同。此画为胡同 7 号，是绍兴会馆。鲁迅曾居此长达七年半，在这里诞生了中国现代文学史上第一篇白话短篇小说《狂人日记》。

No. 7, Nanbanjie Hutong, the Residence of Lu Xun, the Guild Hall of Shaoxing

Nanbanjie Hutong lies in the central part of Xuanwu District, Beijing. The sketch shows No. 7, the Guild Hall of Shaoxing, where famous writer Lu Xun lived for seven and a half years.

2004 年 7 月 29 日

2004年7月26日

米市胡同43号　康有为故居南海会馆

米市胡同位于宣武区东南部，北起骡马市大街，南至南横东街，因有米市而得名。这里多会馆，尤以南海会馆著名。康有为曾长期居住在北跨院的小院里，因当年有七棵树，又称"七树堂"小院，并在此策划了维新变法。

No. 43, Mishi Hutong, the Residence of Kang Youwei, the Nanhai Guild Hall

Mishi Hutong lies in the southeastern part of Xuanwu District, Beijing. The place got its name its rice (mi in Chinese) market. There are also many guild halls around, including one where famous reformer Kang Youwei lived for a long time in the late Qing Dynasty (1644-1911).

2004年8月2～3日

北半截胡同 41 号　谭嗣同故居济阳会馆

北半截胡同位于宣武区中部，北起广安门内大街，南至南半截胡同，成名于明代，称半截胡同。画中是胡同的 41 号，为济阳会馆，即谭嗣同故居。谭在此与康、梁议论变法，并在此被拘捕，后在此停灵。胡同今已不存，但谭嗣同故居被保留了下来。

No. 41, Beibanjie Hutong, the Residence of Tan Sitong, the Jiyang Guild Hall

Beibanjie Hutong lies in the central part of Xuanwu District, Beijing. The sketch shows No. 41, once the Jiyang Guild Hall, also the residence for famous reformer Tan Sitong in late Qing Dynasty (1644-1911).

2004 年 7 月 24 日

[校场胡同三条2号 杨椒山故居]

　　校场胡同位于宣武区中北部，三条北起达智桥胡同，南到校场口胡同。校场三条2号及达智桥胡同12号、14号为松筠庵，原是明嘉靖时杨继盛故居。杨继盛，字仲芳，号椒山，因历数严嵩五奸十大罪，触怒严嵩，受尽酷刑，后被处死。画中是松筠庵内的谏草亭。

No. 2, Jiaochang Hutong Santiao, the Residence of Yang Jiaoshan
Jiaochang Hutong lies in central northern part of Xuanwu District, Beijing. The sketch shows the Jiancaoting Pavilion inside the Songjun'an Nunnery. Yang Jiaoshan was an upright official who was executed by an eunuch for exposing his corruption.

2004 年 7 月 25 日

达智桥胡同 12 号　杨椒山祠

　　达智桥胡同位于宣武区中北部,东起宣武门外大街,西至校场五条,因鞑子桥谐音而得名。胡同 12 号、14 号及校场胡同三条 2 号为松筠庵,原是明代嘉靖时杨继盛的故居,清代乾隆时期胡季堂先生主持在他故居内立祠堂。

No. 12, Dazhiqiao Hutong, the Shrine for Yang Jiaoshan

Dazhiqiao Hutong lies in the central northern part of Xuanwu District, Beijing. A shrine was built inside the Songjun'an Nunnery by Hu Jitang during Qing Emperor Qianlong's reign to commemorate Yang Jiaoshan of the Ming Dynasty, who had once lived here.

2004 年 8 月 16 日

> 山西街甲 13 号　荀慧生故居

　　山西街位于宣武区东北部，北起西草厂街，南至棉花下七条，因传有山西兵营而得名。著名作家张恨水曾在此街的潜山会馆居住。画中是山西街甲 13 号，为著名京剧表演艺术家四大名旦之一的荀慧生故居。

No. 13A, Shanxijie Street, the Residence of Xun Huisheng
Shanxijie Street lies in the northeastern part of Xuanwu District, Beijing. The sketch shows No. 13A along the street, once the residence for Xun Huisheng, one of the four celebrated masters for female roles in Beijing Opera.

2004 年 7 月 25 日

> 金井胡同 1 号　沈家本故居

　　金井胡同位于宣武区中北部，北起上斜街，南至达智桥胡同，因沈家本家门前有金井而得名。沈家本是清末著名法学家，历任刑部侍郎，修订法律大臣等职，他的著作有《枕碧楼偶存稿》、《枕碧楼丛书》等。

No.1, Jingjin Hutong, the Residence of Shen Jiaben

Jinjing Hutong lies in the central northern part of Xuanwu District, Beijing. The hutong got its name from a well (called Jinjing in Chinese) in front of the yard of Shen Jiaben, famous jurist in the late Qing Dynasty (1644-1911).

2004年7月30～31日

| 珠朝街5号　中山会馆 |

　　珠朝街位于宣武区东南部,北起南横东街,西至菜市口大街,原称珠巢街。历史上此街有扬州、云南、中山、成都等会馆,画中是5号中山会馆,原称香山会馆,民国元年孙中山莅此。院内有假山亭桥等。

No.5, Zhuchaojie Street, the Zhongshan Guild Hall
Zhuchaojie Street lies in the southeastern part of Xuanwu District, Beijing. The sketch shows No. 5, the Zhongshan Guild Hall.

三、佛塔、寺庙、道观、教堂
III. Pagodas, Temples, Churches

朝阳门内大街223号　大慈延福宫旧址

朝阳门内大街位于东城区东南部,东起朝阳门立交桥西侧,西至东四北大街南端。大慈延福宫,明成化十七年(1481年)奉旨敕建,是京城明、清两朝著名道观,每年元旦开庙进香举办庙会,香火颇盛。现今仅存东路建筑。

No. 223, Chaoyangmennei Street, a Taoist Temple Originally Built in Ming Dynasty

Chaoyangmennei Street lies in the southeastern part of Dongcheng District, Beijing. There is a Taoist Temple famous during Ming (1368-1644) and Qing Dynasty (1644-1911) times, which hosted temple fairs on New Year's Day every year.

2005年10月14日

禄米仓胡同 5 号　智化寺

禄米仓胡同位于东城区东南部，东起小牌坊胡同，西至朝阳门南小街，因胡同北侧过去有禄米仓而得名。禄米仓胡同东是古老的智化寺，这座古庙为明代宦官王振于 1443 年所建，智化寺因为古老的音乐而知名，从智化寺墙外经过，常能听到僧人们练习演奏佛乐的声音。画中是智化寺山门。

No.5, Lumicang Hutong, Zhihuasi Ruddhist Temple

Lumicang Hutong lies in the southeastern part of Dongcheng District, Beijing. The sketch shows the gate of Zhihuasi Temple.

2006 年 10 月 5～10 日

禄米仓胡同 智化寺万佛阁

如来殿万佛阁一底一楼，是智化寺最大的建筑，除供奉释迦如来本尊外，上下两层山墙上，佛龛满布，内有小佛9999尊，因此得名，其顶部藻井20世纪30年代流失美国。画中是从智化寺西边的小巷进去，即见到红色寺墙内的万佛阁及一株数百年的古柏。

Lumicang Hutong, Palace of Ten Thousand Buddhas at Zhihuasi Ruddhist Temple

Palace of Ten Thousand Buddhas at the bottom and Hall of Buddha on the second floor compose the largest building in Zhihuasi Temple.

2006年10月15～20日

2004年10月12日

砖塔胡同　万松老人塔

砖塔胡同位于西城区中部，东起西四南大街，西至太平桥大街，因东口有万松老人塔而得名。万松老人是金元间名僧，圆寂后葬于此处，砖塔七级，高丈五尺，有石额曰万松老人塔，清乾隆十八年奉敕修九级。砖塔胡同是北京最早出现，且保留其称的胡同。

Zhuanta Hutong, the Wansonglaoren Pagoda
Zhuanta Hutong lies in the central part of Xicheng District, Beijing. The name is the oldest of any hutong in Beijing.

2004年10月11日

砖塔胡同 68 号　关帝庙旧址

　　画中为砖塔胡同 68 号关帝庙旧址，建立年代不详，属私建。山门坐南朝北，门额为"古刹护国关帝庙"。过去每年农历六月二十日砖塔胡同关帝庙要举行庆祝关帝诞辰活动，届时家住附近的信徒都要前来敬香，庙内和尚诵经鸣钟，热闹非凡。

No. 68, Zhuanta Hutong, the Site of the Guandimiao (War God) Temple

Zhuanta Hutong lies in the central part of Xicheng District, Beijing. The sketch shows No. 68, the site of the Guandimiao (War God) Temple.

2004年8月10日

烟袋斜街37号 广福观旧址

　　烟袋斜街位于西城区东北部,东起地安门外大街,西至小石碑胡同,东西斜形走向,旧时多经营烟具的店铺,故得名。画中为街内37号广福观旧址,建于明天顺三年(1459年),坐北朝南,有山门、前殿、中殿、后殿,供奉关帝及玄坛财神及龙王,是保存较好的道教宫观。

No. 37, Yandai ("Tobacco Pouch") Xiejie Street, the Site of Guangfuguan Taoist Temple

Yandai ("Tobacco Pouch") Xiejie Street lies in the northeastern part of Xicheng District, Beijing, getting its name from its many tobacco shops in old times. The sketch shows No. 37, the entrance gate to Guangfuguan Taoist Temple.

白塔寺东夹道 白塔寺

白塔寺东夹道位于西城区中部，南北曲折走向，南起阜成门内大街，北至安平巷，因其地位于白塔寺东而得名。白塔寺原名是大圣寿万安寺，始建于元代，特邀尼泊尔工艺家阿尼哥参加。原来的白塔寺遭受雷击起火，明天顺元年重修后改称妙应寺，俗称白塔寺。

Baitasi Dongjiadao Hutong, the Baitasi Ruddhist Temple

Baitasi Dongjiadao Hutong lies in the central part of Xicheng District, Beijing. Baitasi Temple was built in the Yuan Dynasty (1279 - 1368), originally called Dashengshou Wan'ansi Temple. The Nepalese architect Arniko was invited to help with its design.

2005 年 7 月 6 日

大石桥胡同61号　拈花寺旧址

大石桥胡同位于西城区北部，东起旧鼓楼大街，西不通行，61号院为拈花寺旧址，明万历九年（1581年）建立。原名护国报恩千佛禅寺，清雍正十二年（1734年）四月奉敕重修，赐名拈花寺。此画为拈花寺山门。

No.61, Dashiqiao Hutong, the Site of Nianhuasi Ruddhist Temple

Dashiqiao Hutong lies in the northern part of Xicheng District, Beijing. The sketch drawing shows the gate of Nianhuasi Temple, originally called Baoguo Baoen Qianfo Zen Temple.

2005年10月16日

正觉胡同甲9号　正觉寺旧址

正觉胡同位于西城区东北部，东起棉花胡同，西至新街口南大街。明代称正觉寺胡同，因正觉寺而得名。甲9号院为正觉寺旧址，寺坐北朝南，中轴线依次为：山门、天王殿、大雄宝殿、接引殿，后院有北房三间。此画为正觉寺山门。

No. 9A, Zhengjue Hutong, the Site of Zhengjuesi Ruddhist Temple

Zhengjue Hutong lies in the northeastern part of Xicheng District, Beijing. The sketch shows the gate of Zhengjuesi Temple.

2006年5月27～28日

象牙胡同与天主教堂

象牙胡同位于西城区南部，东起油坊胡同，西至宣武门内大街。相传此处清代曾出土过一只象牙，故得名。从胡同东口向西，即可见到位于宣武门东大街路北的一座北京现存最古老的天主教堂，这座教堂建于明万历二十九年（1601年），是意大利传教士利玛窦创建。

Xiangya Hutong and the Catholic Church

Xiangya Hutong lies in the southern part of Xicheng District, Beijing, getting its name for the discovery of a piece of ivory there. Looking westward from the hutong, on the north side of Xuanwumen Dongdajie Street, there stands the oldest catholic church in Beijing which was founded in 1601 by the Italian Jesuit Matteo Ricci.

2006年8月29～9月3日

2007年6月29～7月5日

前细瓦厂胡同17号 "莲花山下院"旧址

　　前细瓦厂胡同位于西城区南部,东起兵部洼胡同,西至西交民巷。胡同17号为寺庙旧址。门额上写"莲花山下院",据传是袁世凯题写,因袁的亲属在此庙出家。现庙内已成民居。

No. 17, Qianxiwachang Hutong, the Site of the "Lianhuashan Xiayuan" Temple

Qianxiwachang Hutong lies in the southern part of Xicheng District, Beijing. No. 17 yard was the site of a temple with the gate inscription "Lianhuashan Xiayuan" said to have been written by Yuan Shikai.

2004年9月5日

法华寺街65号　法华寺旧址

　　法华寺街位于崇文区中部，东起南岗子街，西至天坛路，因有法华寺而得名。法华寺始建于明代，是北京外城大寺之一，寺中的海棠花很有名。据《行素斋杂记》载："崇文门外法华寺佛殿前后海堂数株，独殿后一株每年春秋两番作花，亦理不可解者。"现寺内已成民居。

No.65, Fahuasijie Street, the Site of Fahuasi Buddhist Temple

Fahuasijie Street lies in the central part of Chongwen District, Beijing. The temple, one of the major temples in the outer city, was built in Ming Dynasty (1368-1644).

2004 年 7 月 31 日

> 法源寺前街　法源寺

　　法源寺前街位于宣武区中部，东起西砖胡同，西至教子胡同。法源寺建于唐太宗贞观十九年，初名悯忠寺，系唐太宗悯东征阵亡将士所建。寺以丁香著名。有以下主要建筑：山门、天王殿、大雄宝殿、悯忠台、净业堂、大悲坛、藏经楼等。中国佛学院设于此。

Fayuansi Qianjie Street, the Fayuansi Buddhist Temple

Fayuansi Qianjie Street lies in the central part of Xuanwu District, Beijing, where the Buddhist Seminary of China is located.

2004 年 9 月 17 日

扬威胡同 9 号　清真寺旧址

　　扬威胡同位于宣武区东北部，北起三井胡同，南至炭儿胡同。此街的南段有"清真礼拜寺"，建于明朝初年，距今有 500 多年历史，寺院现尚有山门和一座勾连搭屋顶的礼拜殿，正门为三座砖砌封火式门楼，上有绿色琉璃脊、灰筒瓦，院内还保存着阿拉伯文碑。

No. 9 Yangwei Hutong, the Site of the Mosque

Yangwei Hutong lies in the northeastern part of Xuanwu District, Beijing. There is a mosque located along the southern section of the street, which was built in early Ming Dynasty (1368-1644), boasting a history of over five hundred years.

四、文化景观、历史建筑

IV. Cultural Landscapes, Historic Buildings and Strutures

2004年10月16日

国子监街 牌楼

国子监街位于东城区西北部，东起雍和宫大街，西至安定门内大街，因国子监而得名。清代时称成贤街，民国以后称国子监。国子监街有四层牌楼，街口的东西两座，额枋曰"成贤街"，国子监左右两座，额书"国子监"。画中即是其中之一。

Guozijian Street, Pailou

Pailou, a kind of traditional Chinese ceremonial archway, are located at each end of the Guozijian Street in the northwest of Dongcheng District. Guozijian Street was called Chengxian Street in the Qing Dynasty, renamed Guozijian in the republican period (1912 - 1949).

2005年7月10日

铃铛胡同　钟楼

　　铃铛胡同位于东城区西北部，东起钟楼湾胡同，西至旧鼓楼大街。铃铛胡同的东口是钟楼，钟楼的四周用六边形的矮墙围绕，类似铃铛。钟楼始建于明永乐十八年，后毁于火灾。清乾隆十年重建，钟楼上悬有铜钟，重约63吨，是我国最重的铜钟。

Lingdang Hutong, the Bell Tower

Lingdang Hutong is located in northwest of Dongcheng District. Opposite its East entrance is the Bell Tower, in which hangs a 63-ton bronze bell, the heaviest bell in China.

炮局头条　监狱旧址

　　炮局头条位于东城区东北部，北起青龙胡同，南至炮局胡同。清乾隆时此地为炮局，为制造大炮的地方。后炮局废，清末又成为监狱。抗日战争期间，此地成为日本侵略者关押中国"要犯"的监狱，在四周围墙中修筑七座碉堡。吉鸿昌在天津被捕被押往北京，监禁在此地。

Paoju Toutiao, the Site of a Prison

Paoju Toutiao is located in the northeast of Dongcheng District, which was the place for producing cannons in the period of Qianlong Emperor, the sixth emperor of the Manchu Qing Dynasty. During the Sino-Japanese War (1937 - 1945), the Japanese invaders used this place as a prison for so-called "Chinese master criminals".

2005 年 10 月 24 日

2004 年 9 月 24 日

地安门外大街 后门桥

位于地安门外大街中段的后门桥即万宁桥，是北京标志性的古建筑，始建于元代，之所以叫后门桥是因为位于紫禁城的后方。万宁桥岸边的一对石雕螭状吸水兽，据说是龙的儿子，好吞水，故雕于桥头以做镇水之用。后门桥很可能是京杭大运河上的第一桥。

Di'anmenwai Street, Houmen Bridge

Houmen Bridge, also called *Wanning* Bridge, in the middle section of Di'anmenwai Street, was built in Yuan Dynasty (1279 - 1368) is a landmark in Beijing

2005 年 4 月 18 日

银锭桥胡同　银锭桥

　　银锭桥胡同位于西城区东北部，北起后海南沿，南至南官房胡同。因胡同北端有银锭桥，故而得名。银锭桥是一座汉白玉桥，位于连接什刹海与后海的狭窄瓶颈之上，因桥形状像一倒扣的银元宝，故名银锭桥。画面上银锭桥的后面有几家清真餐馆，全都是享誉京城的百年老号。

Yindingqiao Hutong, the Yinding Bridge ("Silver Ingot Bridge")

Yindingqiao ("Silver Ingot Bridge") Hutong located in the northeast of Xicheng District got its name from the Yinding Bridge at its north end.

2004 年 6 月 11 日

前海北沿 18 号　会贤堂旧址

前海北沿位于西城区东北部，东起银锭桥胡同，西至前海西街。因位于前海北岸，故称。18 号原为清代礼部侍郎斌儒宅邸，光绪十六年改为会贤堂饭庄，成为当时文人墨客聚会的场所，因有戏台，也是唱堂会的地方。主体建筑为二层楼，大门的门簪上书"群贤毕至"四字。

No.18, Qianhai Beiyan, the site of Huixiantang Restaurant

Qianhai Beiyan in the northeast of Xicheng District is the site of the former Huixiantang Restaurant which began operation in the 16th year of Guangxu Emperor, and became a gathering place for the literary. There was a stage so opera performances could be arranged.

2005年8月14日

兴华胡同13号 辅仁大学校友会

　　兴华胡同位于西城区东北部,东起龙头井胡同,西至德胜门内大街,明代称兴化寺胡同,清末改为兴化寺街。现寺已不存,画中是胡同13号陈垣故居,现为北京辅仁大学校友会办公室。

No.13, Xinghua Hutong, the Furen University Alumni Association Office

Xinghua Hutong in northeast of Xicheng District was called Xinghuasi in Ming Dynasty and Qing Dynasty after the Xinhua Temple, which no longer exists. At present, the Furen University (former Catholic University)Alumni Association Office is located in the house shown.

【西打磨厂街218号　医院旧址】

西打磨厂街位于崇文区北部，东起东打磨厂街，西至前门大街。因有许多打磨铜器和石器的作坊而得名。画中是胡同218号，为解放前日本人开的结核病医院。现在医院旧址已成为民居。

No. 218, Xidamochang Street, the Site of a Hospital

Xidamochang Street in the north of Chongwen District is named for polishing ("damo") of stone and bronze artifacts which took place here. The picture shows No. 218, which was a tuberculosis hospital opened by Japanese before liberation.

2004年10月2日

魏染胡同30号 《京报》馆旧址

魏染胡同位于宣武区东北，北起南柳巷，南至骡马市大街中段，相传胡同有魏姓染坊，故得名。民国年间《京报》创办人邵飘萍居此，又是《京报》编辑部所在地。现编辑部楼房与邵故居仍在。

No.30, Weiran Hutong, the Site of the Editorial Office of Jingbao Newspaper

Weiran Hutong in northeast of Xuanwu District was the site of the editorial office of Jingbao, a Beijing newspaper published during the Republican period. Shao Piaoping, the founder of paper also lived here.

2004年7月28日

五、四合院宅门
V. Gates of Siheyuan Courtyards

2004年7月3日

干面胡同49号——广亮大门

干面胡同位于东城区东南部，东起朝阳门南小街，西至东四南大街。干面胡同东端与禄米仓胡同相接，是去禄米仓运输禄米的必经之地。旧时为土路，车马行走，尘土飞扬，居民戏称为"下干面"，故而得名。画中是干面胡同49号广亮大门，门楼上的清水脊和门前一对上马石，历经岁月的风雨已残缺不全。

No. 49, Ganmian Hutong, the Guangliang Gate
The picture shows the Guangliang Gate at No. 49 of Ganmian Hutong in the southeast of Dongcheng District.

2004年7月20日

细管胡同 11 号——金柱大门

　　细管胡同位于东城区西北部,东起东四北大街,西至北剪子巷。民国时作细罐胡同。画中是胡同 11 号金柱大门,门楼戗檐上有精美砖雕,从古旧的走马板上依稀还能见到当年的彩绘。

No.11, Xiguan Hutong, the Jinzhu Gate
The picture shows the Jinzhu Gate at No. 11 in Xiguan Hutong, northwest of Dongcheng District. It has beautifully carved brickwork under the eaves, and part of the original painting on the woodwork is still discernable

2004 年 7 月 8 日

秦老胡同 35 号——如意门

秦老胡同位于东城区西北部，东起交道口南大街，西至南锣鼓巷。明称秦家胡同。胡同内 19 号是北京著名的四合院，39 号是幽雅的私家园林——绮园，画中为胡同 35 号如意门，其门头的砖雕有多种吉祥饰品图案，挂落板及冰檐雕花卉，望板雕博古，砖雕工艺精细，是难得的如意门精品。

No. 35, Qinlao Hutong, the Ruyi Gate

Qinlao Hutong is located in the northwest of Dongcheng District. No. 19 compound is a famous Beijing Siheyuan, and No. 39 is Qiyuan, an elegant private garden. The picture shows the Ruyi Gate of No. 35.

2004年10月15日

东棉花胡同 15 号——砖雕拱门

　　东棉花胡同位于东城区西北部，东起交道口南大街，西至南锣鼓巷。明代称棉花胡同。在东棉花胡同 15 号院内，有一座砖雕精美的清代建筑拱门，拱门高 5 米，宽约 3 米，从门洞两旁的金刚墙至栏板，均雕刻文字和松、竹、梅，多宝阁等图案，甚为精美。

No. 15, Dongmianhua Hutong, Carved Brick Archway

Dongmianhua Hutong lies in the northwest of Dongcheng District. Inside No. 15 there is an archway beautifully decorated with carved brick, built in the Qing Dynasty.

2005年4月16日

官书院胡同 7 号——蛮子门

官书院胡同位于东城区西北部，东起雍和宫大街，南至国子监街，呈曲尺形。清代称小后井，以巷内有井，位置靠北端。画中是胡同 7 号蛮子门，门楼建在五阶石基上，戗檐上有吉祥砖雕图案，尤以两枚硕大的抱鼓石光泽润黑，引人注目。

No. 7, Guanshuyuan Hutong, the Manzimen Gate

The picture shows the Manzimen gate of No. 7 compound in Guanshuyuan Hutong in the northwest of Dongcheng District.

焕新胡同 21 号——蛮子门

焕新胡同位于东城区西部,呈东西走向,多曲折,它南起北河胡同,西至东吉祥胡同。清代光绪时称火神庙,因此地有一火神庙而得名。画中是胡同 21 号蛮子门,外墙及门楼高峻,下有四层台阶,门两边有一对硕大汉白玉抱鼓石温润光泽,甚为精美。

No. 21, Huanxin Hutong, the Manzimen Gate

The picture shows the Manzimen gate of No. 21 compound of Huanxin Hutong, which lies in the west of Dongcheng District.

2005 年 5 月 2 日

慈慧胡同9号——广亮大门

　　慈慧胡同位于东城区西部，呈东西走向，两端曲折，东起帘子库胡同，西至地安门内大街。画中是胡同9号四合院大门，属道士帽式广亮大门，左右有八字粉墙。院内有独立式一字影壁、垂花门、游廊、月亮门、后罩房一应俱全。

No. 9, Cihui Hutong, the Guangliang Gate

The picture shows the Taoist hat shaped Guangliang gate at No. 9 of Cihui Hutong in the west of Dongcheng District.

2005年4月24日

【前鼓楼苑胡同7号——蛮子门】

　　前鼓楼苑胡同位于东城区西北部，东起南锣鼓巷，西至南下洼子。明代称孤老胡同，因胡同内有大兴养济院而得名。画中为胡同7号，宅门坐北朝南，建在四阶石基上，是门楼高峻的蛮子门，显得极具实力和气派。

No. 7, Qiangulouyuan Hutong, the Manzimen Gate

The picture shows No. 7 compound of Qiangulouyuan Hutong in the northwest of Dongcheng District. Facing south, the Manzimen gate is built atop four steps, making it appear very grand and impressive.

2005年6月13日

102

飞龙桥胡同5号——蛮子门

飞龙桥胡同位于东城区西南部,东起南池子大街,西临劳动人民文化宫。胡同5号是一处200余年的四合院,门楼左右有八字粉墙。大门正前方有一对上马石,左右各配石雕拴马桩,其门楼的门框上配有四个木雕门簪,上刻"惠我迪吉"四字,可谓京城胡同一景。

No. 5, Feilongqiao Hutong, the Manzimen Gate

The No. 5 compound is a Siheyuan with a history of more than 200 years in Longqiao Hutong, southwest of Dongcheng District. Note the horse mounting rocks on either site of the gate.

2006年6月11～15日

103

2005年10月3日

盛芳胡同 1 号——如意门

　　盛芳胡同位于东城区东南部，东起北总布胡同，西至朝阳门南小街。清代乾隆时称十方院，宣统时称什方院。据传胡同中有一座大庙，庙名十方院，故此得名。画中是盛芳胡同1号如意大门，门楣上有多种吉祥饰品图案，挂落板及冰檐雕花卉，望板雕博古，砖雕工艺精细，是北京四合院中不可多得的珍品。

No. 1, Shengfang Hutong, the Ruyi Gate

The picture shows the Ruyi gate of No. 1 compound in Shengfang Hutong, southeast of Dongcheng District. The exquisite carving tiles are a treasure trove of Beijing Siheyuan art.

2005年10月7日

> 北总布胡同 2 号——重檐牌楼门

  北总布胡同位于东城区东南部,北起大雅宝胡同,南至东总布胡同。北总布胡同 2 号原是用建协和医院的余料盖的,系美国石油大王洛克菲勒基金会董事长为其父母所盖,是北京唯一的重檐牌楼式门楼。

No. 2, Beizongbu Hutong, the Double-eave, Pailou Style Courtyard Gate

No. 2 compound of Beizongbu Hutong was built by Rockefeller, American oil magnate for his parents from materials left over from building the Peking Union Medical College Hospital. Located in the southeast of Dongcheng District, it is the only double-eave, Pailou style courtyard gate in Beijing.

| 黄米胡同9号——"半亩园" |

　　黄米胡同位于东城区西部，北起美术馆后街，南不通行，9号院曾是旧京著名的私家园林之一。此处最早是贾中承的宅园，由清初著名戏曲理论家、作家李渔修建。清道光年间，此宅为麟庆所得，并对住宅特别是花园大加修葺，改名"半亩园"。

No. 9, Mihuang Hutong, the Banmuyuan Private Garden

No. 9 compound of Mihuang Hutong in the west of Dongcheng District was one of the famous private gardens in old Beijing. During the years of Daoguang Emperor in the Qing Dynasty, the compound was acquired by Linqing. After much work on the house, and especially the garden, he gave it the name Banmuyuan, or The Half Mu Garden. (1 mu = 666 sq. meters.)

2006年6月24～7月4日

〖 大佛寺东街 2 号——广亮大门 〗

　　大佛寺东街位于东城区西部，呈南北、东西直角形，大佛寺，即普德寺，俗称大佛寺，现尚存部分建筑。画中是大佛寺东街 2 号旧宅院大门，为一带八字砖墙的广亮大门。

No. 2, Dafosi East Street, the Guangliang Gate

The picture shows the old gate of No. 2, Dafosi East Street, on the west side of Dongcheng District, which is a Guangliang gate with angled walls on either side, in the shape of the Chinese character "Ba", which means 8.

2006 年 6 月 18～24 日

汪芝麻胡同53号——如意门

汪芝麻胡同位于东城区西部,东起东四北大街,西至南剪子巷。明朝丧葬活动盛行,做祭祀用的纸马铺很多,此胡同可能是有一汪氏纸马店,因而得名。胡同宽宏,院落整洁,多深宅大院,画中第一个大门是汪芝麻胡同53号如意门,据说汪道函曾在此居住过。

No.53, Wangzhima Hutong, the Ruyi Gate

Wangzhima Hutong in the west of Dongcheng District is famous for its width, neat yards, and plenty of mansions and Ruyi gates.

2006年9月22~24日

什锦花园胡同19号——广亮大门

什锦花园胡同位于东城区西部,东起东四北大街,西至大佛寺东街,胡同东端北侧为适景园,曾为京师著名私家园林。"园曰适景,都人呼十景园",今胡同19号是一座多进四合院,大门两侧为八字门墙,五步台阶,建筑风格相当讲究,有后花园,直通北面的魏家胡同,此宅原为清末礼部尚书溥良的宅院,后为戴笠公馆。

No.19, Shijinhuayuan Hutong, the Guangliang Gate

No. 19, Shijinhuayuan Hutong in the west of Dongcheng District is a compound with several courtyards and a back garden. Its architecture is most elegant.

2006年7月2~8日

2007年7月13～20日

东四八条61号——蛮子门

　　东四八条位于东城区东部，东起朝阳门北小街，西至东四北大街。胡同内绿树成荫，多深宅大院。画中为胡同61号蛮子门，大门开阔，门前一对上马石历经岁月的风雨虽已残破，但仍能见证当年的辉煌。

No. 61, Dongsibatiao Hutong, the Manzimen Gate

The picture shows the Manzimen gate of No. 61, Dongsibatiao Hutong in the east of Dongcheng District, which is lined with green trees and spacious courtyards.

2007年4月14～18日

【板厂胡同 27 号——广亮大门】

　　板厂胡同位于东城区西北部,东起交道口南大街,西至南锣鼓巷,清乾隆时期称板肠胡同,画中是胡同27号,院落三进,垂花门、抄手游廊、月亮门、后罩房一应俱全,广亮大门外的两棵古树已有百年的历史。

No. 27, Banchang Hutong, the Guangliang Gate

The picture shows No. 27 Banchang Hutong, northeast of Dongcheng District, which has a series of three Siheyuan courtyards, and a Guangliang gate flanked by two hundred-years old trees.

2007年7月26～31日

前永康胡同7号——广亮大门

前永康胡同位于东城区东北部，东起北新桥三条，西至北新胡同。明代称永康侯胡同，因永康侯徐忠的住宅在此而得名。画中为7号四合院，是清末民初建筑，门内有八字影壁、屏门、走廊、垂花门、月亮门，在垂花门两侧的抄手廊南墙上有《红楼梦》壁画十幅。院内正房、耳房、厢房均为硬山合瓦顶，各房头上的砖雕极其精致，有刻福、禄、寿的，有刻松、菊、梅的。由正房西走廊处可通西院，现已被砖砌死。

No. 7, Qianyongkang Hutong, the Guangliang Gate

The picture shows No. 7, Qianyongkang Hutong, in the northeast of Dongcheng district, which was built in the late Qing Dynasty.

2004年6月30～7月1日

庆丰胡同 13 号——金柱大门

庆丰胡同位于西城区中部，北起大茶叶胡同，南至安平巷。因胡同内有观音庵一座，旧称观音庵，1965年定今名。画中为胡同13号，是坐南朝北的金柱大门。

No. 13, Qingfeng Hutong, the Jinzhu Gate

The picture shows the Jinzhu gate of No. 13 at Qingfeng Hutong, middle area of Xicheng District.

2004年8月20日

千竿胡同5号——蛮子门

千竿胡同位于西城区东北部,东起前海西街,西至三座桥胡同。清代称箭杆胡同,民国后"箭"谐音为"千"。画中为胡同5号一蛮子门。门楼在高耸的台阶上,显得鹤立鸡群。据说此院是怡亲王第九代溥静后裔居住的地方,以前曾有200多间房子,现在大约只剩20多间了。

No. 5, Qian'gan Hutong, the Manzimen Gate

The picture shows the Manzimen at No. 5, Qian'gan Hutong, in the northeast part of Xicheng District. The gateway stands atop many steep steps, giving it a towering aspect.

2004年10月9日

敬胜胡同 14 号——金柱大门

　　敬胜胡同位于西城区中部,东起自砖塔胡同,几经曲折与小院胡同、四道湾、小珠帘胡同等多条街巷相通,西至三道栅栏北巷。因有显灵宫位于此巷西端不通行,形似口袋,故名口袋胡同,后改称敬胜胡同。画中为胡同 14 号金柱大门。

No. 14, Jingsheng Hutong, the Jinzhu Gate

The picture shows the Jinzhu gate No. 14, Jingsheng Hutong, middle area of Xicheng District.

2004年9月23日

[铜铁厂胡同6号——金柱大门]

　　铜铁厂胡同位于西城区东北部，东起柳荫街，西通松树街。清代光绪年间称铜铁厂，民国时期沿用，1965年改今名。画中为胡同6号金柱大门，高峻巨丽的门楼，磨砖对缝的院墙，说明宅主的身份非寻常百姓。

No. 6, Tongtiechang Hutong, the Jinzhu Gate

The picture shows the Jinzhu gate at No. 6, Tongtiechang Hutong, in the northeast of Xicheng District. The magnificent arch and the fine brick wall shows the owner was no common person.

2005 年 4 月 15 日

西斜街 42 号——垂花门

　　西斜街位于西城区中部，东南起西单北大街，西北至丰盛胡同，自东南向西北倾斜，故称斜街，与东斜街相对，故称西斜街。画中为西斜街 42 号内垂花门，门前的檩、枋上饰满吉祥图案，寓意满堂富贵，福寿延年，美轮美奂。现已不存。

No. 42, Xixie Street, the Ornamental Inner Gate

The ornamental inner gate, purlin in front of the gate, square timber painted with auspicious designs used to stand inside the courtyard at No. 42, Xixie Street, in central Xicheng District.

东福寿里3号——如意门

东福寿里位于西城区东北部,北起兴华胡同,南至地安门西大街。清末称中官房,民国时改叫福寿里。此画为3号如意门,门楼灰砖合瓦,朱漆木门,尤以两枚雕工精细、色泽温润的汉白玉抱鼓石引人注目,是京城保护较好的如意大门。

No. 3, Dongfushouli, the Ruyi Gate

This example of a well-preserved Ruyi gate is located at No. 3, Dongfushouli, in the northeast of Xichang District.

2005 年 8 月 27 日

{地安门内大街35号——西洋门}

地安门内大街位于西城区东北部,北起地安门西大街,南至景山后街,因位于地安门内而得名。画中为35号,是坐西朝东的拱券门,门楼两侧有西式浮雕,是北京少见的西洋建筑风格门楼,现已不存。

No. 35, Di'anmennei Street, the Western Style Arch gate

The picture shows the western style arch gate of No. 35, Di'anmennei Street, in northeast Xicheng District. Facing east with relief on both sides, the arch is of a rare western style of architecture which no longer exists nowadays.

2005年4月28~29日

[文华胡同17号——蛮子门]

　　文华胡同位于西城区中南部，东起佟麟阁路，西至闹市口中街。因位于石驸马街之后，清宣统年间称石驸马后宅，巷内24号为李大钊故居。画中为17号的蛮子门，大门戗檐下残存的砖雕和已风化的门墩还依稀传递着当年的风采。此宅为二进院落，现为民居。

No. 17, Wenhua Hutong, the Manzimen Gate

The Manzimen gate in the picture leads to a compound of two courtyards in Wenhua Hutong, central south Xicheng District.

2006年4月28~29日

西单手帕胡同12号——
蛮子门

西单手帕胡同位于西城区中南部，东起宣武门内大街，西至佟麟阁路。为避重名，因此巷邻近西单，故而定此名，画中为胡同12号，是坐北朝南的蛮子门。门楼高峻古朴，戗檐下雕有工艺精美的吉祥图案。

No. 12, Shoupa Hutong, the Manzimen Gate

The Manzimen gate in the picture is located at No. 12, Shoupa Hutong near Xidan in central south Xicheng District. The gate facing south is carved with elegant auspicious designs.

2006年4月30～5月1日

宝产胡同 25 号——广亮大门

　　宝产胡同位于西城区中部，东起新街口街，西至赵登禹路。明代称宝禅寺胡同，因内有宝禅寺而得名。画中为胡同 25 号，两边带八字粉墙，属道士帽式广亮大门，院内有独立式一字影壁，影壁上还留有"文革"时期毛泽东身着军装的画像。

No. 25, Baochan Hutong, the Guangliang Gate

The picture shows No. 25, Baochan Hutong, south central Xicheng District. The Guangliang gate with walls on either side jutting out in the shape of the Chinese character ba ("8") is also known as the Taoist hat style gate.

2006 年 5 月 6～8 日

新街口头条 8 号——金柱大门

新街口头条位于西城区北部，东起新街口北大街，北至新街口二条。画中为胡同 8 号，是坐南朝北的金柱大门。大门的走马板上刻有春、夏、秋、冬四季花卉，十分精美。

No. 8, Xinjiekou Toutiao Hutong, the Jinzhu Gate
The picture shows a Jinzhu gate facing north, which is located at the No. 8, Xinjiekou Toutiao Hutong, in the north of Xicheng District.

2006 年 5 月 17～22 日

后公用胡同 8 号——如意门

后公用胡同位于西城区中部，东起前公用胡同，西行北折至八道湾胡同。明称供应库胡同，因皇家外供用库在此而得名。清初讹称宫衣库，民国时改称公用库，因巷居北，故称。画中为胡同 8 号如意大门。现为民居。

No. 8, Hougongyong Hutong, the Ruyi Gate

The Ruyi gate in the picture is located at No. 8, Hougongyong Hutong in the middle of Xicheng District. Nowadays, the compound is used as residential dwellings.

2007 年 4 月 4～13 日

正觉胡同5号——如意门

正觉胡同位于西城区东北部,东起棉花胡同,西至新街口南大街。明代称正觉寺胡同,因正觉寺而得名。画中为胡同5号如意大门,清水脊,戗檐和望柱部分有工艺精细的多种砖雕图案。院内为两进,影壁、垂花门、抄手游廊一应俱全。

No. 5, Zhengjue Hutong, the Ruyi Gate

The Ruyi gate in the picture belongs to No. 5, Zhengjue Hutong, in the northeast of Xicheng District.

2006年5月27～6月1日

前细瓦厂胡同11号——广亮大门

　　前细瓦厂胡同位于西城区东南部，东起兵部洼胡同，西至西交民巷，明代因地处细瓦厂前门而得名。因临近中央衙署，故多大宅。画中为胡同11号广亮大门，门楼高峻巨丽，据说此宅曾是清代一品武官之宅，院内有三进院落。现为高级人民法院宿舍。

No. 11, Qianxiwachang Hutong, the Guangliang Gate

The picture shows the Guangliang gate at Qianxiwachang Hutong, in the southeast of Xicheng District. It was said the compound of three courtyards belonged to a top rank military officer in the Qing Dynasty.

2007年6月23～28日

草厂横胡同 33 号——如意门

草厂横胡同位于崇文区西北部，东起草厂十条，横穿草厂九、八、七、六、五、四条，西至草厂三条，因横穿草厂胡同之中而得名。画中为胡同33号如意大门，其望柱部分雕工精美，斑驳的老门上依稀能看到一副对联，"忠厚留有余地步，和平养无限天机"。

No. 33, Caochangheng Hutong, the Ruyi Gate

The Ruyi gate with exquisite carved pillars is located at No. 33, Caochangheng Hutong, in the northwest of Chongwen District.

2007 年 9 月 7～24 日

2005年7月31日

南芦草园胡同12号——
金柱大门

南芦草园胡同位于崇文区西北部，东起北桥湾街，西至青云胡同。这一带历史上多水道，地势低洼，因曾为芦苇塘而得名。画中为胡同12号，门楼坐南朝北，是不规范的金柱大门。

No. 12, Nanlucaoyuan Hutong, the Jinzhu Gate

The picture shows the No. 12, Nanlucaoyuan Hutong, in northwest Chongwen District. The gateway facing north is a rather irregular Jinzhu gate.

长巷二条2号——如意门

　　长巷二条位于崇文区西北部，北起西打磨厂街，东南至长巷五条。此巷形成于明代。画面中的门楼为胡同2号，是坐东朝西的如意门，门楼高耸，磨砖对缝，门楣上还有多种吉祥饰品，望板雕博古，挂落板及冰檐雕花卉，雕工精湛，是不可多得的如意门精品。

No. 2, Changxiang Ertiao Hutong, the Ruyi Gate

The Ruyi gate facing west belongs to No. 2, Changxiang Ertiao Hutong, in the northwest of Chongwen District.

2005年7月25日

2005 年 5 月 17 日

前孙公园胡同 1 号——如意门

　　前孙公园胡同位于宣武区东北部，东起南新华街，西至魏染胡同北口。明末大藏书家孙承泽曾在此居住，其住宅和花园称孙公园。画中为胡同 1 号，其戗檐和望柱雕工精湛，为道士帽式如意大门。

No. 1, Qiansungongyuan Hutong, the Ruyi Gate
The Taoist hat style Ruyi gate shown in the picture is located at No. 1, Qiansungongyuan Hutong, in the northeast of Xuanwu District.

六、胡同民居

VI. Hutong Street Scenes

2005 年 4 月 23 日

后鼓楼苑胡同

位于东城区西北部。北起鼓楼东大街,南至前鼓楼巷胡同,中间多曲折。因为处于前鼓楼巷的背后,故而得名。胡同笔直、连贯,两旁大部分是清代的院落,灰墙土瓦,是典型的北京内城民居。

Hougulouyuan Hutong

Hougulouyuan Hutong in northwest of Dongcheng District is characteristically straight and is lined with old courtyards from Qing Dynasty on both sides, with grey walls and tiles which are the typical inner city dwellings.

2005年5月22日

白米仓胡同

位于东城区西北部。东起东四北大街,西至北剪子巷。明张爵《京师五城坊巷胡同集》称此巷为济阳卫仓,因与济阳卫仓相邻。清乾隆《京城全图》将此巷截为两段,以今箭杆胡同为界,以东称梯子胡同,以西称白米仓胡同,1965年复将二巷合一,称今名。

Baimicang Hutong

Located in the northwest of Dongcheng District, Baimicang Hutong connects Dongsibeidajie Street in the east with Beijianzi Lane in the west.

2005 年 4 月 30 日

{火药局胡同}

　　位于东城区西部。呈东西走向，西端南折，东起火药局六条，南至北河胡同，因曾是火药局所在地而得名。在火药局胡同旁有伽蓝寺，前殿祀关帝，后殿祀毗卢佛。有钟，上铸火药局字。清朝此地有镶黄旗侍卫校场。

Huoyaoju Hutong

Huoyaoju Hutong in the west of Dongcheng District was once the location of the Gunpowder Bureau.

2005年5月6日

> 大经厂胡同

  位于东城区西北部。西起北锣鼓巷，南至鼓楼东大街，北段多曲折，整体呈曲尺形状，相传为印刷经卷场所。大经厂西口旧有大小佛寺胡同，故又相传大经厂为大佛寺，小经厂为小佛寺，曾是晾晒经卷之地。

Dajingchang Hutong

It was said that Dajingchang Hutong in the northwest of Dongcheng District was the place for printing Buddhist scriptures.

2005年6月4日

协和胡同

　　位于东城区东南部。北起东堂子胡同，南至外交部街。清代时称蝎虎胡同。协和胡同皆为平房居民，1号院是一座如意门，门楼坐西朝东，其望柱部分采用的结构为桥样栏杆，有较简单的砖雕图案。

Xiehe Hutong
Located in the southeast of Dongcheng District, Xiehe Hutong runs from Dongtangzi ("East Manchu Temple") Hutong in the north to Waijiaobu ("Foreign Ministry") Street in the south.

2005年10月20日

石雀胡同

位于东城区东北部。东起新太仓胡同，西至东四北大街。清代乾隆时称石桥胡同，宣统年"桥"谐音为"雀"，故称石雀胡同。胡同内幽静整齐，灰砖青瓦，枝叶繁茂的老树，默默地为这里的居民遮阳挡雨。

Shique Hutong

Located in the northeast of Dongcheng District, Shique Hutong runs from Xintaicang Hutong in the east to the Dongsi Beidajie Street in the west.

2006年9月10～16日

[顶银胡同]

位于东城区东南部。东起贡院西街，西至朝阳门南小街。明代称赶驴桥，清代称今名沿用至今。至于顶银胡同名字的来历，一说胡同内旧有打制金银首饰的铺子故称；一说胡同内有做假银锭的黑店，在铅锭外部包上银箔，将银顶在上面，故称顶银。

Dingyin Hutong

Located in the southeast of Dongcheng District, Dingyin Hutong runs from Gongyuan ("Examination Hall") West Street in the east to Chaoyangmen Nanxiaojie Street in the west.

景阳胡同（之一）

　　位于东城区西北部。东起南锣鼓巷，西至豆角胡同。明代称宣家井胡同，清代称井儿胡同。井儿改景阳，当是谐音加喻意。景阳胡同院落宽宏，房屋整齐，中间曲折。画中是胡同7号，院内的影壁还残留有"文革"时期的标语。

Jingyang Hutong (I)

Jingyang Hutong with spacious yards, orderly houses and twists and turns in the middle is located in the northwest of Dongcheng District.

2006年7月15～21日

景阳胡同（之二）

位于东城区西北部。东起南锣鼓巷，西至豆角胡同，中间曲折。其西段是北京著名的私家园林——可园的爬山廊（画中倾斜的瓦顶即是），景观颇为丰富，是北京胡同游中难得的幽静之地。

Jingyang Hutong (II)

This picture shows Jingyang Hutong, which has the famous climbing corridor of Keyuan Gardern, a famous private garden of Beijing, at its west end. The hutong is located in the northwest of Dongcheng District running from Nanluoguxiang in the east to the Doujiao Hutong in the west.

2006年7月10～15日

福祥胡同

位于东城区西北部。东起南锣鼓巷,西至东不压桥胡同,因福祥寺而得名。福祥寺建于明正统元年(1436年),是武姓太监为英宗祝寿舍宅而修。有山门、前、中、后殿,现只有中殿尚存。

Fuxiang Hutong

Fuxiang Hutong is located in the northwest of Dongcheng District running from Nanluoguxiang in the east to the Dongbuyaqiao Hutong in the west.

2006年9月16～21日

> 大菊胡同

　　位于东城区东北部。东起东直门南小街，西至新太仓胡同。清乾隆时称瓦礤胡同，据传此地专出供官府、庙堂所用之瓦，故此得名。清宣统时称瓦岔胡同。胡同内古树成行，枝叶繁茂，掩映着青砖灰瓦的老宅，是难得的幽静之地。

Daju Hutong

Daju Hutong is located in the northeast of Dongcheng District running from Dongzhimen Nanxiaojie Street in the east to the Xintaicang Hutong in the west.

2007年7月21～25日

2004年8月15日

南官房胡同

　　位于西城区东北部。东起前海北沿，西南至毡子胡同。清乾隆《京城全图》中此处称南官府胡同，光绪年间称南官房。南官房胡同61和63号原为圣泉庵。画中是49号一民居，房顶上长满了绿色爬山虎。南官房胡同是一条斜街，为了最大限度的采光，院落的大门与胡同采取一种锯齿形态，从而保持正南正北方向，这在北京胡同中是很少见的。

Nanguanfang Hutong

Nanguanfang Hutong is located in the northeast of Xicheng District running from Qianhai Beiyan in the east to the Zhanzi Hutong in the southwest.

2004 年 9 月 26 日

{小金丝胡同}

位于西城区东北部。北起北官房胡同，南至大金丝胡同，位于大金丝胡同北侧。在清乾隆《京城全图》中称金银丝绦胡同，《光绪顺天府志》称金丝套胡同。宣统时析为两条，根据路面的宽窄，分称大、小金丝套。

Xiaojinsi Hutong

Xiaojinsi Hutong is located in the northeast of Xicheng District running from Beiguanfang Hutong in the north to the Dajinsi Hutong in the south.

2005年4月13日

> 北官房胡同

　　位于西城区东北部。东起银锭桥胡同，西至前井胡同。清乾隆《京城全图》中此处称北官府胡同，光绪年间称北官房。

Beiguanfang Hutong
Beiguanfang Hutong is located in the northeast of Xicheng District running from Yindingqiao Hutong in the east to the Qianjing Hutong in the west.

146

2004 年 9 月 21 日

南玉带胡同

　　位于西城区中部。北起小院西巷，南至兵马司胡同，因胡同走势呈环状故称玉带胡同。民国后为与宫门口附近的北玉带胡同有别，改称南玉带胡同。画中是一户百姓家的小门，在胡同里多见用碎砖砌成的矮墙和静卧在墙角下的石磨盘。

Nanyudai Hutong

Nanyudai Hutong is located in the middle part of Xicheng District running from Xiaoyuan Xixiang in the north to the Bingmasi Hutong in the south.

前公用胡同

位于西城区中部。东起新街口南大街，西至赵登禹路。明代称供应库胡同，因皇家外供用库在此而得名。清初讹称宫衣库，民国时改称公用库，因巷居南，故称。胡同现还依旧保留着古老的风貌。15号四合院原系清末内务府长官崇子原的宅邸。

Qiangongyong Hutong

Qiangongyong Hutong is located in the middle part of Xicheng District running from Xinjiekou Nandajie Street in the east to the Zhaodengyu Road in the west.

2006年5月15～16日

[宫门口头条]

　　位于西城区中部。东起宫门口西岔，西至阜成门北大街。清代属正红旗地界，因地处宫门口西侧第一条胡同，故称宫门口头条。头条中的老墙和宅门还是那么原汁原味，是为数不多的比较规整的胡同之一。

Gongmenkou Toutiao

One of the well-preserved standard hutong, Gongmenkou Toutiao is located in the middle part of Xicheng District running from Gongmenkou Xicha in the east to the Fuchengmen Beidajie Street in the west.

2006年5月3～5日

> 后帽胡同

　　位于西城区中部。东起北帽胡同，西至赵登禹路。明代称帽儿胡同。清代将帽儿胡同分为五个段落，此巷位于前帽胡同以北，故称后帽儿胡同。

Houmao Hutong

Houmao Hutong is located in the middle part of Xicheng District running from Beimao Hutong in the east to the Zhaodengyu Road in the west.

2006年5月13～14日

北海北夹道

位于西城区东北部。北起恭俭二巷，南至高卧胡同。清代末年出现。此巷是一条狭窄的小胡同，其西侧是北海高墙，又因处于北海的北部，故而得名。胡同狭长曲折，老墙高耸斑驳，因少有人知，故为难得的清幽僻静之地。

Beihai Beijiadao

Beihai Beijiadao is located in the northeast of Xicheng District running from Gongjian Erxiang in the north to the Gaowo Hutong in the south.

2005 年 7 月 18 日

大红罗厂南巷

位于西城区东北部。北起大红罗厂,西折至小拐棒胡同。清末称穿堂门,堂指厅堂,如果一座厅堂有前后两门,而且放在正厅的前方用来通行,这样的厅堂便叫穿堂,此巷在历史上也许起过类似作用?

Dahongluochang Nanxiang

Dahongluochang Nanxiang is located in the northeast of Xicheng District running from Dahongluochang in the north and winds its way west to Xiaoguaibang Hutong.

2006 年 9 月 28 ~ 30 日

小拐棒胡同

位于西城区东部。东起大拐棒胡同,北至大红罗厂南巷。拐棒名称很可能是过去胡同的形状类似于猪的小腿,但是由于历史变迁,胡同的有些形状发生了变化,不再具备这个特点了。

Xiaoguaibang Hutong

Xiaoguaibang Hutong is located in the east of Xicheng District running from Daguaibang Hutong in the east and north to the Dahongluochang Nanxiang.

2006年10月1～4日

后细瓦厂胡同

位于西城区东部。东起井楼胡同，西至北新华街。清代称后细瓦厂，因在明代的细瓦厂以北而得名。据说胡同13号为过去在故宫掌管施工建材预算的"算盘高"之宅，因其在施工前对所需建材预算精准，很少浪费，姓高，故人称"算盘高"。

Houxiwachang Hutong

Houxiwachang Hutong is located in the east of Xicheng District running from Jinglou Hutong in the east to the Beixinhua Street in the west.

2007年7月6～12日

[圆宏胡同]

位于西城区中南部。北起天仙胡同，西至闹市口南街。因寺而称。清代称圆宏寺。园宏寺始建于唐，除山门不存外，其余殿宇均在，有四层大殿，被分割为若干院落，现为民居。

Yuanhong Hutong

Yuanhong Hutong in the middle south area of Xicheng District runs from Tianxian Hutong in the east to the Naoshikounanjie Street in the west.

2006年9月4～8日

2004 年 6 月 28 日

大市胡同

位于崇文区西部。北起东半壁街,南至西晓市街。因市场而得名。胡同 11 号即民国初年的"估衣同业公会",后改为民宅。画中的建筑为胡同 20 号,现已不存。

Dashi Hutong

Dashi Hutong is located in the west of Chongwen District running from Dongbanbi Street in the north to Xixiaoshi Street in the south. The building in the picture is No. 20, Dashi Hutong, which no longer exists.

2004 年 9 月 2 日

> 西厅胡同

　　位于崇文区中部。东起三转桥胡同与东厅胡同相通，西至石板胡同。可能是原于东厅胡同旧时有崇南坊的一个巡捕厅衙署，而名东厅胡同。民国后以南河漕为界，其东名厅儿胡同，其西名西厅胡同。狭窄而曲折的胡同里，多为贫民百姓居住的破旧矮小的房屋。

Xiting Hutong

Xiting Hutong in the middle part of Chongwen District runs from Sanzhuanqiao Hutong in the east, connects with Dongting Hutong, and runs on to Shiban Hutong in the west.

2005年6月18日

[薛家湾胡同]

　　位于崇文区西北部。东起北武圣巷,西至北桥湾街。此地明清以来称薛家湾,原为旧三里河拐弯处,相传有一使船的人家姓薛,故名。这一带历史上多水道,地势低洼,故而房屋的地基都高,胡同走向也颇弯曲。

Xuejiawan Hutong
Xuejiawan Hutong in the northwest of Chongwen District runs from Beiwushengxiang in the east to Beiqiaowan Street in the west.

2005 年 6 月 17 日

西八角胡同

位于崇文区西北部。北起薛家湾胡同、南至珠市门东大街。中间有四个曲弯，而且最窄处只有一尺多。明代称巴家胡同，以巴氏人家居此而得名。清代称八角胡同，一以谐音而改，二以此巷形状七转八角之故。

Xibajiao Hutong

Xibajiao Hutong in the northwest of Chongwen District runs from Xuejiawan Hutong in the north to Zhushikou Dongdajie Street in the south.

南翔凤胡同

位于崇文区西北部。北与北翔凤胡同相接，南至西兴隆街。明朝时称此胡同为墙缝胡同，是表示胡同狭窄似墙缝之意。经实地考察，南翔凤胡同最窄处仅二尺多宽。画中的大门为109号，现已不存。

Nanxiangfeng Hutong

Nanxiangfeng Hutong is located in the northwest of Chongwen District, connects with Beixiangfeng Hutong in the north and runs to Xixinglong Street in the south. The gate in the picture belongs to No. 109, Nanfengxiang Hutong, which no longer exists.

2005年7月20日

草厂二条

位于崇文区西北部。北起西兴隆街,南至北芦草园胡同。据清代《宸垣识略》记载,二条内曾有邵武、黄岗、应城等会馆。胡同内多有台阶高耸的宅门,过去这里曾是河道,地势低洼,因而院落的基础都颇为高峻。

Caochang Ertiao Hutong

Caochang Ertiao Hutong in the northwest of Chongwen District runs from Xixinglong Street in the north to Beilucaoyuan Hutong in the south.

2007年6月10～17日

2007年6月2～9日

草厂四条（之一）

位于崇文区北部。北起西兴隆街，南至北芦草园胡同。此画第一个大门为草厂四条南口40号。胡同狭长曲折，因过去这里地势低仄，故房屋的台阶都颇高。

Caochang Sitiao Hutong (I)

Caochang Sitiao Hutong in the north of Chongwen District runs from Xinglong Street in the north to Beilucaoyuan Hutong in the south. Due to the low-lying terrain, the steps in front of the compounds are very high and the Hutong formed is narrow and irregular.

草厂四条（之二）

位于崇文区北部。北起西兴隆街，南至北芦草园胡同。因胡同狭窄，故多随墙门，是外城民居的典型代表。

Caochang Sitiao Hutong (II)

Located in the north of Chongwen District, Caochang Sitiao runs from Xinglong Street in the north to Beilucaoyuan Hutong in the south. Due to the narrowness of the hutong, many gates are built flush with the wall, which is typical of houses in the south part of the city.

2007年8月31～9月6日

2005年6月1日

[草厂五条]

　　位于崇文区西北部。街道呈斜向，北起西兴隆街，南至北桥湾街。胡同内曾有宝庆、仙裕、黄梅会馆。胡同里的树多，夏日午后，树影婆娑，浓荫蔽日，是行人喜欢的去处。

Caochang Wutiao Hutong

In the northwest of Chongwen District, Caochang Wutiao Hutong runs from north to south, starting from Xixinglong Street to Beiqiaowan Street.

2007年9月7日~20日

> 草厂七条

　　位于崇文区西北部。北起西兴隆街,南至北芦草园胡同。胡同内曾有南安、袁州、惠州会馆。在地势低洼的胡同里,普通市民的随墙门,也多建在颇高的台阶上。

Caochang Qitiao Hutong

In the northwest of Chongwen District, Caochang Qitiao Hutong runs from north to south, starting from Xixinglong Street to Beilucaoyuan Hutong. In this low-lying area, people usually built their gates atop several steps.

{草厂八条}

位于崇文区西北部。北起西兴隆街，南至薛家湾胡同。胡同内曾有辰沅、汉阳会馆。胡同幽静古朴，人车稀少，强烈的日照，摇曳的树影，展现出一片老北京清凉夏日的景色。

Caochang Batiao Hutong

Caochang Batiao is located in the northwest of Chongwen District running from Xixinglong Street in the north to Xuejiawan Hutong in the south.

2007年5月19～22日

草厂九条

位于崇文区西北部。北起西兴隆街，南至薛家湾胡同。曾建有蕲州会馆。画中的建筑是草厂九条14号，磨砖对缝并带砖雕的如意大门，在草厂一带显得格外气派。

Caochang Jiutiao Hutong

Caochang Jiutiao is located in the northwest of Chongwen District running from Xixinglong Street in the north to Xuejiawan Hutong in the south. The imposing. No. 14 compound has walls built with polished bricks and a Ruyi gate decorated with brick carving.

2005年6月7日

2004年6月29日

| 草厂十条 |

　　位于崇文区西北部。北起西兴隆街,南至薛家湾胡同。胡同内曾有湖南、湘潭、长沙、京山、长郡等会馆。画中的建筑为草厂十条3号,画中面容安详的老人,坐在家门口悠闲地纳着凉,看着过往的行人,与熟悉的老街坊打着招呼,这是老北京胡同内常见的场景。

Caochang Shitiao Hutong
Caochang Shitiao is located in the northwest of Chongwen District running from Xixinglong Street in the north to Xuejiawan Hutong in the south.

2007年4月21～24日

{群智巷}

位于崇文区西北部。街巷呈"人"字形，东口北口通南芦草园胡同，西口至大江胡同。其街巷的形状似马尥蹶子，故在清代《京师坊巷志稿》中记为南缺子胡同，民国时改为"南缺孜"。这里地势低仄，过去曾是河道，故房屋多建在高高的石基上。

Qunzhi Lane

Located in the northwest of Chongwen District, Qunzhi lane branches out in a "Y" shape, like the Chinese character "Ren" (People). Its east and north entrances are connecting to Nanlucaoyuan Hutong, while its west entrance leads to Dajiang Hutong.

清华街

位于崇文区西部。东起磁器口大街,西至鲁班胡同。因清化寺而得名。2000年扩建两广大街时部分拆除。清化寺建于明宣德七年(1432年),明正统九年(1444年)寺庙建成。明正德七年(1512年)毁于火,次年再建。今寺庙已废。

Qinghuajie Street

Qinghuajie gets its name from Qinghua Temple located in the west of Chongwen District. The hutong runs from Ciqikou Street in the east to Luban Hutong in the west.

2007年5月10～18日

得丰东巷

位于崇文区西北部。东起大席胡同，西至小席胡同。清代此地名元帝庙，因此巷西北段有玄帝庙而得名。巷东段以前叫十间楼，后改今称。这里民房古朴，灰砖青瓦，绿树成荫，曲径通幽。画中第一个门为胡同61号，磨砖对缝的老墙上还残留着"文革"时期的标语。

Defeng Dongxiang

Defeng Dongxiang, called Yuandi Temple in Qing Dynasty, is located in the northwest of Chongwen District.

2007年10月9～21日

銮庆胡同

位于崇文区西北部。东起南深沟胡同，西至长巷三条。明代时称銮敬胡同，据说是以平民命名的胡同。胡同内原有襄阳、粤西会馆，胡同的9号是广西会馆。

Luanqing Hutong

Luanqing Hutong is located in the northwest of Chongwen District running from Nanshen'gou Hutong in the east to Changxiang Santiao in the west. No. 9 compound is the Guangxi Guild Hall.

2007年6月18～22日

> 小席胡同

位于崇文区西北部。呈丁字形,东起大席胡同,西北至得丰东巷,西南至大江胡同。因靠近芦草园,多有用苇草编席的作坊,又连接大席胡同,既短又窄,因而得名。传说这一带多为豆腐作坊,门前的石碾、石磨盘是过去磨粮食做豆腐用的,废弃后多用以保护房基,也是胡同一景。

Xiaoxi Hutong

Xiaoxi Hutong is in the shape a "T", or the Chinese character "Ding". It is located in the northwest of Chongwen District running from Daxi Hutong in the east. It is said there were many tofu mills in the area. The grindstones in front of the gate once used to make tofu are now used to protect the foundation of the house.

2007年9月25～10月8日

2004年6月24日

东北园北巷

位于宣武区东北部。北起刘家胡同，南至东北园南巷。清代此地是菜园，又位于琉璃窑的东北，故得名。琉璃窑是为宫廷和寺庙烧制琉璃砖瓦之处。在琉璃厂东北侧垦荒种蔬菜，供琉璃厂官吏和窑工吃菜。画中的建筑为北巷7号，门楼左侧的院墙上还镶有拴马桩。

Dongbeiyuan Beixiang

Located in the northeast of Xuanwu District, Dongbeiyuan Beixiangruns from Liujia Hutong in the north to Dongbeiyuan Nanxiang in the south. The picture shows No. 7 compound of Dongbeiyuan Beixiang with a place to tie horses on the wall to the left of the gate.

2004年9月13日

百合园胡同

位于宣武区东北部。东至延寿街，西至东北园南巷。清代光绪年间称百花园。据说，这里曾经有花园，种有花草树木，供人游览欣赏，民国时将"花"改为"合"。这里胡同幽深，闹中取静，依旧保留着古老的风貌。

Baiheyuan Hutong

Baiheyuan Hutong located in the northeast of Xuanwu District was called Baihuayuan during the reign of Guangxu Emperor in the Qing Dynasty.

2004年7月24日

[达智桥胡同]

位于宣武区中北部。东起宣武门外大街，西至校场五条。因鞑子桥谐音而得名。此街河南会馆即嵩云草堂，也是举人聚集签字的地方。嵩云草堂是道光年间河南显宦袁甲三创建的，清末是强国会活动场所。画中的建筑为胡同55号。

Dazhiqiao Hutong

Located in the central north part of Xuanwu District, Dazhiqiao Hutong was the He'nan Guild Hall, a place where Juren(successful candidate in the imperial examinations at the provincial level during the Ming and Qing dynasties) gathered.

176

2004年9月16日

铁门胡同

位于宣武区东北部。北起西草厂街，南至骡马市大街。因有圈虎的栅栏而得名。此处有三多：酱菜铺多，其中以桂馨斋、兰馨斋为著名。井多，胡同内有井七十二眼。历史名人多。画中的建筑为胡同 17 号，现已不存。

Tiemen Hutong

Tiemen Hutong located in the northeast of Xuanwu District runs from Xicaochang Hutong in the north to the Luomashi Street in the south. The area is famous for its 72 wells, its pickle shops and its celebrities.

177

2005年4月29日

[校场小五条]

位于宣武区中北部。校场小五条是校场口数条胡同中的一条，南北走向。明清时期校场口一带为操练比武之场所，此处多是窄小曲折的小胡同和寻常朴素的随墙门，是典型的宣南民居。

Jiaochang Xiaowutiao

In the middle north of Xuanwu District, Jiaochang Xiaowutiao is one of the Hutongs of Jiaochangkou area which was a drill ground in the past.

2004 年 10 月 20 日

培英胡同

位于宣武区东北部。东起煤市街，西至棕树二条。因在此胡同居住的京剧名家王瑶卿培养出众多的京剧名演员故而得名，"四大名旦"和"四小名旦"等都曾受教于此。画中的建筑为胡同 25 号，门楼上的砖雕雕有多种精美的吉祥图案，门前还有一对拴马石桩。

Peiying Hutong

A famous Peking Opera performer lived in Peiying Hutong, in the northeast of Xuanwu District. He also trained up many famous performers. The picture shows the No. 25, with a pair of hitching posts in front of the gate.

2005年5月19日

梁家园东胡同

位于宣武区东北部。北起梁家园北胡同,南至骡马市大街。这条小巷中间一段被堵死后,很难被人发现。画中的大门为胡同4号,中西合璧的拱券门楼上有精美的荷花荷叶砖雕。

Liangjiayuandong Hutong

The picture shows the No. 4 compound of Liangjiayuandong Hutong in northeast of Xuanwu District with a Chinese and Western fusion style arched gate which was decorated with beautiful lotus leaf carvings on its bricks.

2005年5月23～24日

前孙公园西夹道

位于宣武区东北部,北起后孙公园胡同,南至前孙公园胡同。明末大藏书家孙承泽曾在前孙公园居住,其住宅和花园称孙公园。此巷幽深狭长,灰砖青瓦的院墙,还保留着原汁原味的古老风貌。

Qiansungongyuan Jiadao

The west narrow lane of Qiansungongyuan Jiadao is located in the northeast of Xuanwu District running from Housungongyuan Hutong in the north to the Qiansungongyuan Hutong in the south. The narrow lane is flanked by grey tile walls.

取灯胡同

位于宣武区东北部。东起煤市街，西至扬威胡同。明代时命名的取灯胡同是因胡同里有很多家"取灯"（指引火柴物）的库房。胡同内有多处下洼院落，画中的第一处建筑为胡同中 25 号，即是一处下洼院。

Qudeng Hutong

Qudeng Hutong is located in the northeast of Xuanwu District running from Meishi Street in the east to Yangwei Hutong in the west. In the past, there was a warehouse for storing tinder (Qudeng).

2007 年 4 月 25～28 日

红线胡同

位于宣武区东北部。北起前孙公园胡同，南至骡马市大街。明、清以来一直称麻线胡同。京剧表演艺术家杨宝森曾居此胡同。夏季的红线胡同被浓密的槐树遮掩着，显得斑驳凉爽，老北京的素美在这里体现得淋漓尽致。

Hongxian Hutong

Hongxian Hutong is located in the northeast of Xuanwu District running from Qiansungongyuan Hutong in the north to Luomashi Street in the south.

2005 年 6 月 26 日

2005年7月2日

粉房琉璃街

位于宣武区东南部。北起骡马市大街,南至南横东街。原称粉房刘家街,当系做粉条的刘家住此故名。此街两侧国槐成行,枝叶繁茂,三三两两的老人最喜欢在这样的树荫下乘凉。夏季凉爽的粉房琉璃街,也为行人喜欢的去处。画中的大门为胡同65号。

Fenfangliuli Street

Located in the southeast of Xuanwu District, Fenfangliuli Street runs from Luomashi Street in the north to the Nanhengdongjie in the south. The gate in the picture belongs to the No. 65.

兴胜胡同

位于宣武区东北部。北起后孙公园胡同，南至前孙公园胡同。因兴胜寺而得名。兴胜寺又名兴盛寺，明代建。庙内原有明天启二年（1622年）所铸的铜钟，清康熙辛巳（1701年）进士汪士竑书写"禅径清闲"匾额。今寺已废。画中为胡同12号的门楼。

Xingsheng Hutong

Xingsheng Hutong located in the northeast of Xuanwu District runs from Housungongyuan Hutong in the north to the Qiansungongyaun Hutong in the south. The picture shows the gate of the No. 12.

2005年7月15日

北大吉巷（之一）

位于宣武区东南部。东起果子巷，西至米市胡同。因打劫巷谐音而得名。明时称打却巷，清称打街巷，清末谐音雅称大吉巷。画中为胡同中段。狭长的胡同多是青砖灰瓦的院墙与碎砖砌成的矮墙，是典型的宣南民居，现已不存。

Beidajixiang Lane (I)

Beidajixiang lane, which has dwellings typical of southeast Xuanwu District, runs from Guozixiang in the east to the Mishi Hutong in the west.

2006 年 5 月 23～26 日

北大吉巷（之二）

明代称打却巷，清代改称大吉巷，1965年定今名。胡同内曾居住过多位梨园名家。画中为胡同东段。这里的房屋大多破旧矮小，是平民百姓的住宅，寻常朴素的色调充满了整条胡同。

Beidajixiang Lane (II)

Most of the houses in Beidajixiang belong to common folk, and are shabby and low, ordinary and simple.

2006年7月22～26日

2007年4月28～5月1日

> 排子胡同

位于宣武区东北部。东起三富胡同，西至大宏巷。清代末年出现，至今未变。据说，旧时此处住有习武之人，经常练举双石，双石成排放置，后来成为胡同的名称。画中第一个大门为胡同47号。中西合璧的随墙拱券门，其门楼上的葫芦形砖雕与众不同，内雕吉祥花卉图案，雕工精湛，现门楼还在，砖雕已无。

Paizi Hutong

Paizi Hutong is located in the northeast of Xuanwu District running from Sanfu Hutong in the east to Dahongxiang in the west. The first gate in the picture is that of No. 47, with a fusion of Chinese and Western styles.

掌扇胡同

位于宣武区东北部。东起前门大街，西至煤市街。由"张善家胡同"谐音而得名。据说在明代这条胡同居住着一户姓张的大户，经常施舍为善，人称此胡同为"张善家胡同"，清代乾隆年间改名为"掌扇胡同"。

Zhangshan Hutong

Zhangshan Hutong located in the northeast of Xuanwu District runs from Qianmen Street in the east to Meishi Street in the west.

2007年5月6～9日

七井胡同

位于宣武区中部，在烂缦胡同与西砖胡同南端之间，南通南横西街。清代时这里有七口井，因而得此名，现井已不存。走进胡同，格外空灵清净，胡同10号的院墙上还残存着"文革"时的标语，烙印着那个年代的记忆。

Qijing Hutong

Qijing Hutong in the central area of Xuanwu District got its name from the seven wells it had in the Qing Dynasty, which no longer exist.

2007年8月2～9日

广安后巷

位于宣武区北部。北起老墙根东口,南至定居胡同。因后坑而得名。此巷在司家坑东侧,故名后坑,系垃圾集中地。后填坑,建房住人。1965年改今名。这里的胡同曲折幽静,是典型的外城民居。

Guang'an Houxiang

Guang'an Houxiang with typical dwellings is located in the north of Xuanwu District, and runs from Laoqianggen Dongkou in the north to the Dingju Hutong in the south.

2007年8月10～21日

南大吉巷

位于宣武区东南部,东起果子巷,北至北大吉巷,向南为死巷。明代称羊肉胡同,可能与屠羊售羊有关。旌德会馆曾在巷内。画中的建筑为南大吉巷10号,磨砖对缝的老墙及门楼上精美的砖雕,都将成为记忆。

Nandajixiang

Nandajixiang is located in the southeast of Xuanwu District, and runs from Guozixiang in the east to the Beidajixiang in the north and to a dead-end lane in the south.

2007年11月3～9日

> 贾家胡同

位于宣武区东南部。北起果子巷，南至南横东街中段。明代时称贾哥胡同。清代时"哥"谐音为"家"，称贾家胡同。胡同57号为阎王庙，门额尚存"古刹地藏禅林"字迹，是供奉地藏菩萨的庙宇。画中的建筑是胡同66号，带有东洋风格的建筑。

Jiajia Hutong

Jiajia Hutong is located in the southeast of Xuanwu District, and runs from Guozixiang in the north to the middle section of Nanheng Dongjie street in the south. The building in the picture is No. 66, which has a Japanese flavor.

2007年10月22～11月2日

保安寺街

位于宣武区东南部。东起果子巷,西至米市胡同。因有保安寺而得名。因岁久浸废,保安寺今只存一殿。保安寺街多会馆,现存五处,以街东端湖南湘潭会馆最著名,胡同中古树掩映的老宅,将要永远地消失,但它却留在了我的画本里,残存在记忆中。

Baoansi Street

Baoansi Street gets its name from Baoan Temple which is located in the southeast of Xuanwu District. The hutong runs from Guozixiang in the east to Mishi Hutong in the west.

2007 年 11 月 10 ~ 24 日

 # 胡同写生日记选编
Selected Diaries on Hutong Sketching

跨车胡同（2004年8月25日）

　　早饭后走路到单位，中午又乘车去了护国寺，准备画护国寺西巷及西配殿。到后发现寺巷还在，配殿已无，残墙裸露。一打听才知道，几天前一场大火烧毁了寺内的西配殿，据说此建筑已有700年历史了，望着废墟懊悔不已，但也只能接受现实了。我在护国寺周边转了转，拍了寺内仅存的金刚殿和其他几处建筑。

　　从护国寺出来，我又去找跨车胡同，寻找齐白石故居。沿着太平桥大街南行，一路上打听了三次，最后是一名建筑工人回头指向南面一片工地告诉我说："还有一处平房的那就是跨车胡同。"我带着忐忑不安的心情急忙走过去一看，跨车胡同已无，眼前是一座老宅子，孤零零的被高大的楼房包围着，墙上有齐白石故居的文保牌。见此景我是既高兴又失落，高兴的是白石老人的故居还在，失落的是此处已没有了老北京那种胡同幽幽小巷深深的味道了。

　　我坐在故居的正对面观察着，故居是15号，门楼是典型的蛮子门，其顶部的清水脊蝎子尾缺了一个角，红黑相间的木门上腐朽了几个小洞，大门紧闭，不知院内是什么样。我正画着，故居的门忽然打开，从里走出三个人，是院主人送两位客人。送走客人后，院主人见我在画故居走过来笑着问："怎么不画领导的宅子？"我一愣，知道他是在开玩笑，我也笑着说"都要画"，随后向他询问了故居的情况，得知跨车胡同早已消失，只保留下15号院，这里是白石老人在北京住的时间最长的院落。故居是一座三合院带跨院的住宅，坐西朝东，三面平房，一面围墙，院里有三间北房，是整个庭院的主体，为两明一暗，正屋为客厅，西为卧室，东为"白石画室"，还有东西厢房，现住在这里的是白石老人的后人。

我很喜欢白石老人的绘画，其笔墨简洁到近乎于童趣，留出的大面积空白给人以想象的空间。我今天的写生也仿效了白石老人的风格，只画故居的门楼，舍弃两边的墙，留出大面积的空白，突出了故居的主体，画得还比较令人满意。在写生时边上有个排雨水的地沟，蚊子很多，身上被叮了几个大包，这也是常事。

我带着收获的喜悦走出那条白石老人曾走过无数次的小路，边走边回首，来到了车水马龙的大街上，走出很远，再回首，故居已隐没在了一片喧闹中。（见54页）

西四北三条（2004年8月7日）

今早出来，乘52路，转22路到缸瓦市下车，准备去砖塔胡同的张恨水故居写生，见故居已拆，又去西四北三条的程砚秋故居写生。走进胡同西口不远，就见到路北39号墙上镶着程砚秋故居的文保牌，故居为如意门，大门紧闭，故居东边现在开了一家发廊，与故居很不协调，我想画面上避开，但构图不好，只能照此画了。

今天很闷热，中午阳光直晒，我贴着墙根儿坐下，但还是晒着半边身子。画到一半时，故居的门打开，出来一位60多岁的老人，见我在画故居，走过来很慈祥地问我："喝水吗？"我忙说："带着呢，谢谢！"接着我向老人询问了故居的情况，老人很随和，让我到院里看看。我收拾好画本随老人进了院，一进院门立刻凉爽了许多，见迎面是一个大影壁，上有青翠的爬墙虎，方正的院子里正房和倒座房各有四间，院里还种着石榴树。老人说："这是程先生亲手栽下的。"老人又带我穿过月亮门，走进后院，后院有三间北房，里屋为卧室，外屋两间分别是程先生的书房和练功房，名"御霜簃书斋"，现陈列着程先生生前用过的戏装、剧本、图书等物品，陈设依旧，整个院落显得宁静、典雅、质朴，充满了艺术气息。我对京剧基本上是外行，但程派那深沉含蓄、低回婉转又柔中有刚的唱腔常让我陶醉，尤其是他在抗日期间曾荷锄务农的事迹常常使我敬仰。

从故居出来，我向老人道谢，继续写生，随着心中肃然起敬之情，故居之形也就跃然纸上。今天喜忧各半，喜的是有缘进故居参观，忧的是写生时从空中飞过一只喜鹊落下的鸟屎正掉在画本上，影响了画面。（见52页）

棉花胡同（2004年8月19日）

早饭后走路去公司，上午设计一本画册。下午2点从公司出来，乘车去西城区棉花胡同寻找66号蔡锷故居。厂桥下车，走护国寺街，找到棉花胡同一直向北。见66号门前有两棵老槐树，一粗一细引人注目，墙上没有故居的文保牌，问一老人，说此宅即是蔡锷的故居。

我在故居对面的商店前坐下，观其故居，是一个极普通的如意门，院墙之下堆放着一些垃圾，门楼上的水泥大瓦是后补的，看上去有点别扭，若不是门前那两棵古槐，难以使人注目。据胡同里的老人讲这两棵古槐已有200多年的历史了。

在写生时，有一位中年人路过和我攀谈起来，交谈中得知他是美术老师，他说从小就住在这条胡同，除蔡锷故居外，还有一处老宅在胡同南口路西的地方，原来是大太监李莲英的宅子，20世纪70年代初他还曾到过那里，看到院子北面有五开间的大北房，雕梁画柱，院后有花园，后来院子施工听说还挖出水井和金佛等。临走这位老师非常客气地建议我"用线再肯定一些，画面会更有精神"。我向他道了谢。

写生完，我走进蔡锷故居，这是一所二进院落，外院有北房、南房各三间，倒座房五间。内院与外院间被一道走廊相隔，内院有北房、东西房各三间，房屋由廊、抄手游廊和回廊相连形成一体，房屋的基本格局仍在，只是凭添了几许沧桑。据住在院里的老人讲此宅原来是天津盐商何仲璟的私宅，后来因蔡锷将军居住此地而变得丰富，斗转星移，物是人非，虽早已逝去了往日的风采，但小院深藏的历史确让人产生无限的遐想。（见51页）

小杨家胡同（2004年8月20日）

早饭后乘车到西城区新街口大街，找"小羊圈胡同"。沿着平安大街向北拐，顺路东走不多远就是小杨家胡同，入口只有一米多宽，很不起眼。沿着狭长窄小的胡同拐了几个弯后，是一片小空场，走到胡同南侧东南角的一个小门是小杨家胡同8号，那就是老舍先生的出生地。很普通的小门是后盖的，房子也大多不是原先的故宅，院内一棵枣树，枝杆扭曲地向外伸展着，饱含着岁月的感怀。墙上没有文保牌，我询问了在这里遛儿的老人，得到了肯定的回答后，便在小空场的一个大石盘上坐下，找好角度开始写生，因上午太晒没有画完，准备下午再画。

我沿着弯弯曲曲的小巷继续寻找着，眼前巷陌中的院落，灰皮剥落的院墙，枝干扭曲的老树，忽然让我想起了老舍笔下许多作品里都有这些胡同的影子，小羊圈胡同已融进了老舍先生的作品中。不知不觉地走出了胡同，来到护国寺街的梅兰芳故居，故居正在装修，也没法画，我又继续向南，走到千竿胡同，发现一个很气派的蛮子门，建在很高的石阶上，有些鹤立鸡群。这里正在修路，我坐在斜对门的一户石阶上写生，有位路过的老人告诉我说："此宅现是怡亲王后裔居住，从前有200多间房，现在只有20多间了。"画到一半时，遇到一位推着自行车，也在胡同里寻找"目标"的同行，我们聊了一会儿各自画胡同的经历，得知他是做舞美的，平时没有任务时就在胡同里画油画。他看了我的写生后，建议我可以多画一些胡同，我也有同感，正准备从画门楼向胡同转变。

画完千竿胡同大门后，已5点多。我依然沿原路走回老舍故居的小杨家胡同，夕阳在树间已融成了一片绯色。我一口气把老舍故居画完，心情非常愉快，今天天气很热，画得也很辛苦，但辛苦的付出换来的是收获的喜悦。且喜悦之心是无法用语言形容的，回家的路上回想着今天走过的胡同，仍历历在目。（见49页）

丰富胡同（2004年8月21日）

早饭后乘车到灯市西口，沿街西行，走到丰富胡同，紧临胡同南口的19号就是老舍的故居。故居大门坐西朝东，是典型的墙垣式门楼，朴实无华，两扇黑漆木门紧闭，墙上镶有老舍故居的文保牌。

我沿着胡同向北又走了一段路后，没有发现太多的门楼，又回到故居前，坐在故居斜对门的台阶上开始写生。不一会儿天阴了下来，接着就掉下了雨点，我躲进故居斜对面的门道内，边避雨边画，雨大了，风带着雨点刮到画本上，树上的叶子也随风落了一地，有一阵儿雨下得特大都把胡同下白了。我坐在门道内独自享受着这难得的雨景，等我写生完毕，雨也停了。

走出胡同，我来到故居前的书店，这里有许多老舍先生的作品和老北京胡同的书籍，我看了一会儿书然后购门票，进故居参观。故居东侧为一小院，只有两间平房，西边是个狭长小过道，北侧是一座普通的三合院，走进院门，绕过影壁是直通正房的甬道，院里正房三间，左右各带一间耳房，分别为客厅、卧室和书房，现保持原状陈列，东西厢房三间，现都成为纪念展室，分别陈列着老舍先生各个时期的手稿、照片和实物等，从6个方面展示了老舍先生不平凡的一生。置身院中，房屋依旧，树木依然，院中种满了花草，其中有两棵柿子树让人驻足，这是老舍先生亲手种植的，老舍夫人胡絜青还给小院起了个雅号叫"丹柿小院"。

走出故居，在外徘徊很久，注目着这平凡普通的院落，想象着那动乱岁月，心情却是无法平静，39年前老舍先生从此院走出，就再也没有回来。（见48页）

朱茅胡同（2005年5月11日至12日）

11日。今早走路到前门外的朱茅胡同，这条胡同9号名为"聚宝茶室"，是解放前"八大胡同"的妓院旧址，现已是民居了。此建筑与众不同，从外表看是个三围二层的建筑，大门集中西风格于一身，砖垛装饰与拱形门洞是西式风格，门顶部是伊斯兰风格，中间雕有"福禄"二字，大门外左右各盖了一个小煤棚，看上去有点别扭。

去年就想画此宅，但因胡同窄、建筑高、构图不好画，故没有画成。今天我是坐在斜对门的门道内，上午起好构图，中午饭后，下午又接着画。听院内住户讲，此门已不是原来的老样子了，这是三年前拆了又新盖的，与原门不大一样，原门是老式木门，两侧还有门墩，墙也是仿照过去的样子砌成的，我听后感觉有点遗憾，但所幸院内还保持原样。下午我走进院内，本不大的院落又盖了小厨房，显得更窄，但基本格局未变。抬头见一二层的木制镂花挂檐板与围栏廊柱上的雕饰还都齐整完好，就连走雨水的水漏也同样完好，这已是很难得了。今天画到下午5点也没画完，明天再去。

12日。今早还是走路到朱茅胡同，继续画"聚宝茶室"，从上午9点画到12点终于画完，据住在这里的人说，"聚宝茶室"有许多人来画过，而我画的时间最长也最细。（见28页）

中午我又乘车去了北新桥的九道湾社区，因昨天见晚报刊登了一位67岁老人正在社区举办"北京民居画展"，今天特来参观。到了九道湾社区不仅看了展览，并有缘见到了画者郑希成老人。郑老的画是用白描形式从另一个视角去表现北京的四合院和胡同，让人眼前一亮。我让郑老看了我的胡同写生，他很高兴并让我到他家去做客。我随老人到了九道湾胡同的家，老人很随和直率，给我讲了他这几年为留下这些宝贵的胡同、四合院所经历的一些事，让我很震惊。我也与郑老讲了我画胡同的经历，老人说自己年龄大了，腿脚也不方便，希望多一些年轻人做这项工作，并鼓励我继续把胡同画下去，郑老还介绍我参加胡同保护的民间活动——"爱泼斯坦90北京胡同地名文化遗产保护工程"研讨会。

今天的收获是开扩了视野，增加了信心，还多了一种史命感。

东四四条（2005年5月29日）

今天早上准备去东四街道一带去写生，走到东四四条，从东口进入，快到西口时发现一座老式铺面二层小楼，我驻足观看，门牌是86号，一层大门两侧似有字，已看不太清了，二楼上设阳台，阳台底部为铁艺牛腿，饰镂花挂檐板，装饰性很强，（注：笔者在2007年，再次路过此地，见小楼已经整修一新，大门两侧对联也重新露出面目，对联似有禅趣，我用笔记下"镜里人是一是二，笛中意至妙至神"，门楼上方的横匾写着"恒昌瑞记"，下方还有"照相""洋货"等字。）一看便知是一家老店铺。我问了路边一位老住户，说此楼原来是日本人设计的，曾经是一家有名的大饭庄。

在画的过程中，有两个推着自行车路过的人见我在写生，停步看了我正在画的和以前的写生，还询问我在东四一带画有多少幅。通过与他们攀谈得知他们一位是东四街道的袁主任，与另一位工作人员出来办事，袁主任说，他们正准备要出一本介绍东四街道历史文化的书籍，想通过文字、照片和绘画等素材表现，希望我能帮着多画一些东四街道的老建筑。临走还留了我的电话，说要再与我联系。

下午画完，我走到外交部街等胡同寻找新"目标"。走过协和胡同，来到东堂子胡同我的母校二十四中，见东堂子胡同路北的墙上写着许多的拆字，看来东堂子胡同风貌不久也要有大变化了。（见4页）

钱市胡同（2005年8月4日至6日）

4日。今早6点出来，走到大栅栏珠宝市街，找到钱市胡同。钱市胡同与喧嚣的珠宝市街相比显得闹中取静，如不注意很可能擦肩而过。这条胡同是北京最窄的胡同，两个人行走也需错身才行，往上看是一线天。这里曾是清代著名的金融街，现在已经很少有人知道了。

两个月前的6月6日我曾到过此地拍照，那天遇到胡同中的谢先生，见我在拍照，请我到他家去看看。我随他进了家门，让我很吃惊，连厨房不到八平米的小房里住了三口人，屋里几乎没有活动的空间，屋和厨房之间还有一线天，谢先生说是做饭排热气的，下雨又往屋里流水，雨下大了，只能往外淘水，他说在这里已经住30年了。今天我来胡同写生，又遇到了谢先生，见我在画胡同，他说上次以为我是记者或是拆迁的呢。

今天上午画得很有感觉，昨天有朋友建议我要注意画面的虚实对比，有些应大胆地舍，今天起稿很小心，特别注意了虚实关系。中午公司来电话说明天有人要找我设计。

5日。今早继续到钱市胡同写生，画到10点钟停笔回公司去做设计。

6日。今早还是到钱市胡同，今天在这里画了一天，前两天在此认识的街坊也熟了，我边画边与她们聊天。胡同北侧的这家住着一位老太太，一听说话就是地道的北京人，老人告诉我她家住的这房子墙体是磨砖对缝的。我停笔仔细观看，摩挲着那一块块古老墙砖，确实工艺精湛，这在北京老宅中也不多见，因为这里没有什么人来，所以保护得非常好。老人还请我到她家里做客，我随老人进了房间，屋内并不大，与老人一样干净利落。老人说："去年有两个清华大学建筑系的学生来过，研究过房子的建筑，说是做毕业论文用。"我不懂建筑，但感觉这房子与众不同而又中西结合，值得研究。

下午有位老住户告诉我说："钱市胡同里共有9组建筑，多是当年的银号和银票的管理机构用房。"我沿着胡同，由东向西数着，发现南侧有5个三合院平房，北侧有4个中西结合的二三层小洋楼，从墙上的石匾上还依稀可辨认出"万丰银号"的字样。我走到胡同尽端，见平房后面还有一庭院，上面有座硬山起脊的罩棚，往里走有些暗，据说这就是清末做银钱交易的场所。

我问老住户："这里为什么是死胡同？"老人说："这是因为过去是金融机构，怕偷。"

今天这幅画完成后，老街坊们都说画得非常细，太像了，我也感觉还可以。前一段时间素描主要是虚实和取舍不好把握，看见的东西太多，舍得不够，虚实对比也不够，这幅画从一开始就注意了这两点，故感觉还可以。

临走，我向这里的老街坊们道谢，他们都希望我有时间再来，我也很想再来画画胡同西侧那座硬山起脊的老建筑。（见26页）

飞龙桥胡同（2006年6月11日至15日）

11日。今早8点就到了南池子，找到飞龙桥胡同5号。这个门楼我在照片上见过，因不知地址，一直也没找到，还以为拆了呢。前几日在画正觉胡同时遇到一位同行，告诉我此地有一个门楼，保护得还不错，让我来画。今天见到实景，喜出望外，正是我要找的那个门楼。此大门为蛮子门，与众不同的是门楼两侧有八字粉墙，左右还配有石雕拴马桩，上透雕圆形古钱币图案，红漆大门有些斑驳，两侧的门墩已被砸毁，有些美中不足，门框上配有四个门簪，上雕文字"惠、我、迪、吉"，门楼两侧的墙砖上还残留有"文革"时期的标语"毛主席万岁"和"中国共产党万岁"，尤以大门前一对长方形的汉白玉石墩引人注目。

我在大门前寻找着角度，大门的对面是个公厕，东侧有一棵老槐树，旁边是几个垃圾筒，为了构图的需要，我只有在公厕与垃圾筒两个位置二选其一了，选来选去还是决定坐在厕所内画大门的正面，最能表现气势恢弘的宅门。为了画好此幅画，我做好了长时间的准备，今天用了半天多时间，只把构图定好，为了使画面有一种神秘感，我特意把大门半遮半掩地留了一个缝。此地离天安门不远，是寸土寸金之地，因不容易发现，故少有人来，闹中取静，在此写生也真是一种享受。

13日。今天阴预报说有小雨，我还是去了飞龙桥胡同，在写生时，雷声不断，但雨始终没下。胡同内三三两两的老住户边聊着边看我写生，据他们说以前溥仪的姑姑曾在此宅居住过，还有的说是皇亲或是在故宫掌事的人住过，再后来是一位国民党的官员曾住此，改革开放后还从台湾回来看过此宅，说法不一。现在院内是高级法院的宿舍。我向老住户询问了门墩的去向，他们说是"文革"时破四旧砸毁了，还说院里原有游廊和月亮门也已拆了。一位中年人告诉我说："门前两侧的汉白玉大石墩不是上马石，原来上面有一对石狮子，后来这对石狮子不知道去向了，只留下了这一对石墩座，外人都以为是上马石呢，因为上马石一般都是有台阶的，而这一对石墩是平的。"听他这么一说，还真有些道理。

14日。今天在凉爽幽静的环境下画了多半天，主要是在门楼和门前的两个石墩做了深入的刻画，其次是八字粉墙和拴马桩，墙上的标语也有意地强化了，使画面有恢弘、沧桑、神密和时代感。

15日。今天是这幅画的收尾和调整，我用了半天时间把画面的树和整体的黑白灰做了调整。画到中午，有位住在胡同里的老先生从家里拿了一壶水让我喝，他说看我每天在这画太辛苦了。我向老人道了谢。我在胡同里写生，经常遇到好心人的帮助，很让我感动！

这幅画我用了5天时间终于画完，和往常一样，画完后我也是到院里去拍了些照。走进5号大门，迎面是独立的一字影壁，院子很大，是两进院落，院里有枣树和杨树等多种树木，有正房、东西厢房和后罩房，房屋高大轩敞，灰砖、红绿相间的门窗古朴中不失华丽，只是院中盖了些小房，听院里人说，要不是"非典"可能就拆了。我拍完照后从5号出来，还应邀到胡同11号小院做客，此院是私宅，院里有10多间房，院内没有盖小房就显得院中规范而干净。据院中主人讲，三年前民间保护胡同的华新民女士也来此院看过。（见103页）

薛家湾胡同（2006年7月28日至8月1日）

7月28日。早6点起，7点就到了薛家湾胡同，这一带我很熟，每天上下班都要经过这里，胡同正在准备拆迁改造，大部分住户都已搬走，还有些私家房主没有搬。

胡同 39 号为钱氏宗祠，是钱氏的家庙，大约有 200 年的历史，院内居住着一些钱氏的后人。钱氏宗祠门楼不大，门框有些凹陷。门额上雕有"钱氏宗祠"四个大字，两扇木门上的字迹已被风雨剥蚀得看不太清。

　　有位 50 多岁的钱氏后裔告诉我说："祠堂的老门牌是 4 号，后改为 39 号。木门上的字迹上联是'武肃勋铭久'，下联是'彭城世泽长'，横楣是'铁券家声'。"他还从家里拿出一张发黄的青年报让我看，上边有一张钱氏后人在门前的合影以及介绍钱氏宗祠的文章。聊了一会儿他说带我到院里看看，我随着他走到门前，他指着凹陷的门槛说："原来的门槛是汉白玉的，'文革'后被人盗走了。"走进小院，地面明显低于街面，院内又加盖了许多小房，显得潮湿而拥挤。他说："院落是三进院，前院曾经是祠堂，原供有钱王像和康熙题写的'保障江山'匾额和道光年间重修时刻下的石碑等文物，大多已不知去向，中院供奉钱氏夫人的牌位，后院是花园。"现在院中大部分钱氏后人已搬走，因年久失修显得破败不堪。从院出来，他告诉我说，不久他也要搬走，因为这里要改造。

　　我坐在 48 号门前开始写生，正画着从门里出来一位大姐，见我坐在门口画着，吓她一跳，可能是把我当拆迁办的了。我赶紧给她让道，并说明我是画胡同的，以前也遇到过这种误会。据胡同的人讲此宅是前门布巷子里一老商号的私宅，从外表看并不起眼儿，原来是殷实人家。

　　8 月 1 日。这几天我每天都来写生，而 48 号的大姐也每天推着自行车出来进去的，后来熟悉了，得知这里住着她的母亲，她是每天来给母亲做饭的。今天早上她告诉我说，前年有个摄影的要前来拍她家的院子，拍完后不久，又回来还想再拍她没答应，她跟我说："想拍照可随时进院来拍。"我心里一喜，我正想要看看小院呢。我谢过大姐后说一定去。下午画完后，正好大姐又推车回来，我与大姐一起进了大门。这个院落是坐南朝北的，大门在西北角，门道不宽，有些暗，但砖雕影壁前一棵盘根错节又枝繁叶茂的金银藤让人眼前一亮，可谓一景，转过影壁，院里方方正正的非常的规矩，是标准的一进院，院内有两棵大树，一棵是枣树，另一棵是椿树，都是枝繁叶茂，院中还有主人种的各种花草，郁郁葱葱、异卉幽芳。

　　院内正房、东西厢房和倒座房都原汁原味，保存完好，房前的廊柱、门窗古色古香，朴实自然。

　　老人坐在正房前正在乘凉，看上去有八十多岁了，身体还很硬朗，我与老人打过招呼，老人也很随和与我聊了一会儿，为了不打扰老人休息我按下快门，把这院中的美景记录下来留在了相机里，也留在了我的记忆里，留待以后慢慢地欣赏。拍完后我向老人和大姐道谢后走出小院，把门又带好，见门上一副对联，上联是"栽培心上地"，下联是"涵养性中天"。（见 56 页）

布巷子胡同（2006 年 8 月 12 日至 16 日）

　　12 日。今早去崇文区布巷子写生，这里正在拆迁改造，胡同内已没什么人了。这一带我很熟悉，童年时母亲经常带我来姥姥家，路过这里有时买些布料或毛线。记忆中那时巷子里有许多卖布匹和针织毛线的店铺，其中一家是很有名的老商号"益记"号布庄，就在巷中间，其建筑是中西结合式的，与众不同，现在仍保存完好。布巷子是南北走向，中间与大江胡同相交，其把角的建筑上还留有"文革"时的标语，烙印着那个年代的记忆。

　　我坐在大江胡同北侧的把角处写生，今天天气闷热又晒，大约十点钟，我坐的地方就开始晒了，画到中午晒得不行了，下午更晒，只好收笔。头一天只起了个稿，构图还比较满意，主要突出了老字号的建筑，其次是把角墙上的标语也留在画面中，这些时代的烙印现在已不容易见到了。

今天有位住在大江胡同还没搬的王先生告诉我，在小江胡同北口有个院子是个老建筑，很有特点，还带我去看了。院子是一个三围二层的小楼，现已人去楼空，王先生说此宅是院落式铺面房，上世纪20年代为"德源金店"，后易主同仁堂，是民国时期的典型商用铺面房。我见小院整体建筑毓秀隽永，大气不凡，具有北京传统的地方建筑特色，可惜今天没带相机。随后王先生还请我到他家去看看，房子不太大有些杂乱，从王先生的话里得知，他是一名律师，现正在为搬迁而打官司，今天在大江胡同里还遇到几户同样因搬迁打官司而没搬的住户。

13日。今天早晨阴有雨和风，雨停后我背着包带上相机，又来到布巷子，今天不晒又凉爽画得也顺畅，本想多画些时间，可画到中午笔没水了，只好收笔，我随后拿着相机去拍小江胡同1号的铺面房。走进院中发现原来院内是四面建筑形成天井布局，北、东、西三面为三个单体重楼式建筑，南面为便于院内采光，只有7间平房。我沿陡峭的木制楼梯上了楼，二楼走道以回廊相连，梅花廊柱间垂挂檐花板，下有菱形倒挂楣子。回廊转角处有垂柱相接，从二层平视远方，尽收眼底的是鳞鳞合瓦的屋顶和郁郁葱葱的树木。拍完照后走出小院，沿小江胡同往南，这里的住户基本上都搬走了，路边的野草开始疯长，有的房拆了开始在修建，远处还有一处阳平会馆旧址也在修缮，不知以后什么人才能住在这里。

下午回到家后又下起了中雨，我睡了一觉，连日的写生疲劳一扫而光。

16日。昨天到公司去设计没来布巷子，今天天气晴好，蓝天白云，难得的好天。我一大早就来到布巷子，今天心情不错，我把余下的画完，调整了画面的虚实关系，有些做了大胆的取舍，总的感觉还可以，今天还拍了布巷子里老墙上的标语和老店铺上的砖匾什么"蚨丰"号、"益记"号等。因为对这里太熟了，很有感情，常会触景生情，现在这一带要拆建改造了，有些眷恋，只能把这些老记忆留下来，待以后细细地品味。（见15页）

取灯胡同（2007年4月25日至28日）

25日。今天早上走过宣武区杨梅竹斜街、扬威胡同、延寿寺街、北火燃胡同、炭儿胡同和取灯胡同，最后是取灯胡同的一处低洼院让我停止了脚步。以前也走过此处，不知什么原因这里有些院门是下洼的而有些又不是，很有特点。我要画的这个院是25号，比较有代表性，门楼明显比路面低。我走下台阶穿过门道，边走边下台阶，向左拐进入院内。院里比院外更低了，院内有北房、南房和东西房，房屋因年久失修显得有些破旧，东西房前又加盖了小房，显得院落窄小。院里很安静没人出来，我没法问只好沿原路走出，见对面20号出来一位大妈，我上前去询问，大妈说这片儿还有几处院落也是下洼院，但每个院下洼的深度不一样，比如她们院和东边的一个院下洼的深度要高于23号四合院，说不清为什么，只是说路面越修越高。

26日。今天在取灯胡同25号画了多半天，因风太大，路上没有什么人，也没有问出个究竟。

27日。今天一早就到了取灯胡同，有位推着车的老先生路过，见我在画胡同，看了一会儿问我："画的胡同发表过吗？"我说"没有"，他说他收藏了很多北京胡同速写，虽然不会画但是很喜欢。我向老先生询问这里的房子为什么有些是低下去的，老人说："这是下洼院，这一带像这样的院子很多，比如耀武胡同也有几处，可能是过去盖房用的砖是就地取材，用院里的土烧制而成，故成了下洼院。"我问："那院里不会存水吗？"老人说："院里的排水系统是通畅的，不会存水。"老先生还告诉我说，他住在廊坊二条，姓郭，过去廊坊头条是灯画一条街，是做宫灯的，天安门的灯就是华美斋定做的。二条是珠宝玉器一条街，还有锦盒等，他家是做锦盒的，今天出来就是给客户送锦盒，路过此地见我在写生胡同,很喜欢。老先生临走前还邀请我有时间到他住的胡同去画并请我到家做客,我谢过老先生说一定去。

28日。今天下午画完取灯胡同25号下洼院后,我又去了耀武胡同。走到胡同中间见到一处下洼门,一看门牌是21号。我走下台阶穿过门道,进院一看是一个又小又窄的院落,房屋有些破旧,东侧还有一个小院门。我穿过细长的门道,见里面还有一个后院也同样是不大而破旧,院内有几户人家,很安静。我拍了照后又沿原路出来,见门口一位老人,我上前询问,老人说:"这儿还有几处是同样的院落",一指旁边的23号门说:"这院也是一处下洼院。"我从外表没有看出,老人说:"你走进去就知道了。"我走进23号门,果真是一处下洼院落,原来这23号门楼是后盖的,把下洼的门楼和台阶挡在里面,故从外表看不出。我走下台阶穿过门道,进到院内,这是一个很小的四合院,正房是坐北朝南,还有倒座房和东西厢房,房屋有些破旧,但依稀还能传递着过去的辉煌。院内正好有位住户在修车,我打过招呼,随后询问院内的历史。此人告诉我说:这是他家的私房,早先盖这房时院落与街道是同样高的,但后来家家都往外倒烧过煤的渣土,日久天长胡同就变得比院内高了。"我问:"那为什么有些院不是下洼的呢?"他说:"那可能是后盖的房,院落地基都加高了。"我不知这种说法是否正确,也算是一家之说吧。(见182页)

七井胡同(2007年8月2日至9日)

2日。今天早上去南城的法源寺一带寻找胡同写生,这里的胡同仍保留着宣南的古老风貌,有些胡同还可见到一些老旧的标语,如包头章胡同就有一宅门的门联是"听毛主席话,跟共产党走",还有一处我记不清哪条胡同了,是个二层简易楼,在楼的侧面墙上也有语录,只是历经风雨,字迹看不太清了。最后我走到七井胡同,见胡同10号是一座老门楼,门前还有一对像上马石一样的高台阶,可能是起保护门楼做用后砌的。遗憾的是门楼和墙面新粉刷不久,已失去了岁月的沧桑,但墙上还隐约能见到"文革"时的大标语,我想画这个门楼并复原墙上的标语,但字迹看不太清。我环顾四周,见胡同南不远处有棵大梧桐树下几位老人在歇凉,我走过去向老人们询问10号院墙上的标语,老人们说,"文革"时墙上就有了标语,当时10号院是街道居委会,那时在门口还开过批斗会,被斗的人在门前低头认罪的样子印像还在,只是墙上的标语老人们众说不一,记不清具体内容了。

我走回10号门前,找好角度先开始画构图,等有人知道墙上标语的内容再补上。我坐的地方没有树荫,上午就开始晒,画到中午实在太热了,只好停笔,中午饭后我在胡同漫无目地转悠着,我走过林荫密布的西砖胡同,曲折静谧的莲花胡同,可能与法源寺很近的缘故,走在这些胡同里显得很清静,同时胡同的意境也显露得淋漓尽致,等到下午2点左右不晒了,才回来继续写生。

8日。今天一早直接来到七井胡同写生,早上凉爽可多画些时间。这几天我写生周围总围着一些人,今天也一样。他们都是这里的住户,有的给我送水,有的给我送苹果,让我非常感动。我边画边与他们聊天,他们说等我画完后一定要拍照留做记念。

下午从10号院出来一位中年人,手里还拿着相机,上来先给我拍了几张照,然后过来说:"见你在这画好几天了,今天过来看看!"我向他询问了墙上的标语是否还记得,我说很想把它复原。他说:"巧了,刷墙那天我无意中拍下了老墙的原貌,本想留个念心儿,这回用上了。"我心惊喜,忙问:"还能找到照片吗?"他说:"存在电脑里了,马上回去调出来。"院主人回去后,我就在外面边画边等候,过了一会儿,院主人出来拿出一个U盘,给我说让我去洗。我收拾好画本,出了胡同口找到洗照片的地方,洗照片的说要等到第二天上午才能取。

9日。今天上午先到七井胡同取回照片，见照片上的标语十分清晰，左侧墙上的大标语是"高举毛泽东思想伟大红旗奋勇前进"，右侧墙上的小标语是"一定要照党中央……"和"念念不忘阶级斗争"等字，大门两侧还各有一块水泥砌的黑板把标语盖住一部分，估计黑板是后砌的。上午我先把门楼两侧墙上的标语复原，下午调整画面，这幅画我用了一周的时间，今天终于画完。这些天非常热，每天挥汗如雨，又怕蹭脏了画面，画得非常谨慎，一周的辛苦换来的是收获的喜悦。

下午我还应邀去了10号院，院主人先拍了我画的这幅"修复"的胡同留做纪念，并请我到正房做客。院主人告诉我说，这院是他家的私房。"文革"前他家是开照相馆的，落实政策后房子又归还了原主。院内有北房、南房和东西房总共10多间，现在院里住着一大家子人，但房子还是不够住的，又在院中盖了两间小房，他就住在其中一间。院主人对我画胡同的经历很感兴趣，又给我介绍了一些老胡同，聊了会儿我向院主人道谢告辞。

走出小院向南出胡同口，这里离法源寺很近，我走进法源寺的山门，寺内暮鼓晨钟，正赶上晚课时间，大殿内诵经声庄严肃穆，我的心好像回到了清静的佛境，恍若隔世。我羡慕住在古刹周边的人们，他们的生活伴随着暮鼓晨钟，是那样的恬静而神秘，古刹已融入了胡同居民的生活，成为胡同独特的风景。其实红尘与静土本就一心。（见190页）

保安寺街（2007年11月10日至24日）

10日。上午在公司做设计，下午背着包，来到宣武区保安寺街。因为这一带要拆迁了，很多住户都已搬走。胡同里很冷清，墙上隔不远就画着白色的圈写着拆字。胡同西口还有个寺庙的山门，但大门已被砌成墙盖成了小房，只有山门的戗檐上那精美绝伦的砖雕还依稀传递着曾经远去的寺庙气息。继续往胡同中走，见胡同中还有几个老宅门被老槐树掩映着，这些色彩斑驳的老门，精致的砖墙，破旧的石鼓门槛，让我感觉好像走进了历史。其中胡同17号门楼最为高大而有气势，我本想进院内看看，却被坐在门洞的老人阻拦了。我理解老人的心情没有做解释，我选择了画17号大门和胡同，但门楼西侧的院墙上被拆了个大洞，也只能在画面里"修复"了。今天画了两个多小时，因为天气太冷只好收笔。

19日。前两天在公司设计没来，今天本想多画些时间，可画到中午刮起了大风，胡同里尘土飞扬，大风把树上的叶子吹得漫天飞舞，因为太冷只好收笔。我在空旷的胡同里漫无目的地走着，脚下踩着被吹落的黄叶。想到无路可走的我与走头无路的胡同，好像有着相同的宿命，心理不禁一阵悲凉。

20日。今天天气非常好，阳光灿烂，共画了5个小时，因久坐在背阴的地方写生，脚和手冻得已不听使唤，直打哆嗦。中午吃了带的面包和一袋奶，边吃边活动着僵硬的身体。这是今年我最后一次在外写生，因为太冷，我画得比较慢，也很谨慎，画面的明暗、虚实、主次、疏密关系处理也很小心，今天还把院墙上被拆的大洞也"修复"成原样。

23日。今天又是个好天，从早10点画到下午3点，因画得过于专注，中午也忘记吃饭了，但还是没画完。下午在胡同里遇到了摄影的张先生，他是我在画细瓦厂胡同认识的朋友，今天又在这见面了。我们边走边聊，来到米市胡同，听胡同老人讲37号曾是旧时棺材铺，据说这里是北京最后一个没有拆的棺材铺旧址，因为此地离过去的杀人刑场菜市口很近，所以才有了这个买卖。其门脸为柏木结构，顶部撅头拍子下面的木制护檐板上刻有文字，上写"自置四川建昌荫陈金丝楠木樟套建香杉江西饶州兜行各省花板一概俱全"。我们走进院里，因正在拆迁，院内很杂乱，有的房子拆了，证明房主已经搬走，但多数还住在此院。院里有一位老人说离此不远有一处值得拍照的老字号，说着就带我们出了院，向北走了一段，有个不起眼的小巷，老人让我们顺此过去就见到了。我们走进窄小又曲折的小巷，拐了两个弯后是一个二层小楼，沿石阶上了二楼。住在二楼的一位老者说，这里是最早的便宜坊旧址。我环视这砖木结构的二层小楼，还依稀地感觉到是个老店铺的样子，只是年久失修，有些破旧不堪了。老者说原来的牌匾在二楼挂着，老便宜坊有200多年的历史了，老者还说文物局的人来过，但是否保留说法不一。我们拍了照后向老人道谢，下了楼又来到北大吉巷。张先生说47号门有一对云纹门墩是北京仅有的两对云纹门墩之一，西城区还有一对，但"文革"时破坏了。拍完门墩我们又沿路往东走，发现这条胡同有许多门墩都很有特点，但这时天渐渐地黑了，圆圆的月亮挂在胡同东口的上空，幽静美丽的胡同像是童话一般。想到这里的胡同可能很快要消失了，心里不禁有些悲凉，我只有把这美景深深地留在记忆中。

24日。上午用了半天时间调整了画面的虚实对比和黑白灰的层次，使画面显得更有精神了。这幅画共用了9天时间，我在胡同写生了4年，这幅画就像是4年的总结考试一样，画得很小心谨慎，因保安寺街这一带的胡同正在拆迁，很快就要消失了，最后这几幅是我"抢"出来的，我把它们留在了我的画本里，心中多少还有些欣慰。

天太冷了，明年再出来。（见194页）

主要参考引证书目

北京地名典　王　彬　徐秀珊主编（修订版），中国文联出版社，2008年11月。